中華新漢民國大總統孫文之像

DR SUN YAT SEN
FIRST PRESIDENT OF THE REPUBLIC
OF CHINA.

Sun yat sen

SUN YAT SEN

AND THE AWAKENING OF CHINA

By

JAMES CANTLIE, M.A., M.B., F.R.C.S.

Dean of the College of Medicine, Hong Kong (1889–1896)

AND

C. SHERIDAN JONES

ILLUSTRATED

New York   Chicago   Toronto

Fleming H. Revell Company

London   and   Edinburgh

[1912]

New York: 158 Fifth Avenue
Chicago: 125 N. Wabash Ave.
Toronto: 25 Richmond St., W.
London: 21 Paternoster Square
Edinburgh: 100 Princes Street

PREFACE TO THE THIRD EDITION

SINCE the issue of the first edition, affairs in the Far East have moved apace. The prophecies of disaster which amounted, and still amount, in some quarters to almost a fetish have proved false; nothing the would-be " authorities " can say or do will serve to put back the clock in China. Sun Yat Sen was, and still is, the *bête noire* to many who knew China in the old days; and their stereotyped remark when his name is mentioned is that " Sun is an idealist," and therefore to be regarded as a man of no consequence. The Chinese do not think so; Sun is to them a deliverer; his head is impressed on the coinage of the country and on the commemoration stamps of the foundation of the Republic.

Dr. Morrison's reassuring letter to *The London Times* did much to sweep away the crude opinions and false beliefs that had been raised abroad concerning the reformed China. Men who knew only the old conditions did their best to wreck China's good name, to stop her monetary credit, and to thwart her progress. An attempt was made to set North against South, and to foment bad feeling between Yuan-shi-kai and Sun Yat Sen. Never was an attempt so completely frustrated. Sun visited Peking at a time when such a step was regarded as amounting to certain death, and many friends tried to dissuade him from going there. Such an impending calamity could not deter Sun when the welfare of his country was at stake. Instead, however, of having to face death, he was well-nigh overwhelmed by kindness and greeted with supreme honor. The streets he travelled through, on his way to the palatial dwelling provided for him, were lined by soldiers, and choirs of children sang songs of welcome. The Manchu Dowager-Empress requested to be allowed to decorate his residence by gifts from her palace, " so that Dr. Sun Yat Sen's stay in Peking should be as pleasant as possible." Neither sacred nor secular history records a more marked triumph. The Royal Family he displaced were the first to honor him; the head of the State accorded him a reception which an emperor might envy; and the people have taken him to their hearts as their national hero.

I therefore make no apologies for, nor withdrawals from, the so-called exaggerations which I have been charged with making concerning Sun Yat Sen. Rather do I apologize for the way in which China has been dealt with by my countrymen and others. When a kindly hand might have been extended to help a people struggling to be free and when the infant State was in jeopardy, instead of helping to make the rough places smooth, the Government of China were harassed by questions concerning loans, frontiers, and suzerain rights. The traditional goodwill and mutual respect which up to almost the present moment have existed between China and Britain have been strained, and it remains to be seen how long it will take before the ill-feeling created will be overcome and confidence restored. The part played by Sun in China during the past twelve months claims further admiration, and it is difficult to exaggerate the meed of praise which must be accorded to one who has proved himself to be perhaps the purest patriot in history.

JAMES CANTLIE.

WAS SUN YAT SEN A UNITED STATES CITIZEN?

WHILE the author of this volume, Dr. Cantlie, was under the impression that Dr. Sun Yat Sen was a native Chinese, born in the province of Kwang-tung, in a remote village situated between the city of Canton and the Portuguese colony of Macao, some thirty miles south of Hong Kong, this statement has been not only questioned, but his American citizenship confirmed by such documentary evidence as would seem to remove all doubt, the publishers having received from Honolulu certified copies of documents which at least appear to be conclusive, as will be seen in the following pages:

DEPOSITION OF HAWAIIAN BIRTH OF SUN YAT SEN.

Adult No. 25

Territory of Hawaii, ⎫ ss.
Island of Oahu. ⎭

(Photograph.)

I, SUN YAT SEN, being first duly sworn, depose and say that to the best of my knowledge and belief I was born at Waimano, Ewa, Oahu, on the 24th day of November, A. D. 1870; that I am a physician, practicing at present at Kula, Island of Maui; that I make my home at said Kula; that my father, Sun Tet Sung, went to China about 1874 and died there about eight years later; that this affidavit is made for the purpose of identifying myself and as a further proof of Hawaiian birth; that the photograph attached is a good likeness of me at this time.

(Signed)   SUN YAT SEN.

Subscribed and sworn to before me this ninth day of March, A. D. 1904.

(Signed)   KATE KELLEY,

(Seal.)   Notary Public First Judicial Circuit.

This is to certify that I have made a thorough examination of the statements made here and am satisfied as to their accuracy; that the photograph attached is a good likeness and that the signature was made by the applicant.

(Signed)   A. L. C. ATKINSON,
Secretary of Hawaii.

CERTIFICATE OF HAWAIIAN BIRTH.

Adult No. 25

 Territory of Hawaii, } ss.
 Office of the Secretary. }

To all whom these presents shall come—Greeting:

This is to certify that SUN YAT SEN, now residing at Kula Maui, T. H., whose signature is attached, has made application No. 25 for a Certificate of Birth.

(Photograph.) And that it appears from his affidavit and the evidence submitted by witnesses that he was born in the Hawaiian Islands on the 24th day of November, A. D. 1870, and that the photograph attached is a good likeness of him at this time.

In testimony whereof the Secretary of the Territory has hereunto subscribed his name and caused the Seal of the Territory of Hawaii to be affixed.

 (Signed) A. L. C. ATKINSON.

Done in Honolulu this 14th day of March, A. D. 1904.

Signature SUN YAT SEN. (Signed.)

FOREWORD

SEVERAL publishers within the last six months have favored me with a request that I should write an account of Sun Yat Sen and his work. I felt honored by their doing so, but being diffident of my ability to accomplish the task, and not having sufficient time at my disposal, I most reluctantly had to decline, and it was not until there was promised me the valuable help of Mr. C. Sheridan Jones that I was able to entertain the idea.

To the excellent chapters contributed by Mr. Sheridan Jones I have only been able to add my personal experiences, and to tell something of the character and career of Sun Yat Sen, and the nature of the arduous struggle in which he engaged. For twenty-five years my wife and myself have had the privilege of a close and intimate acquaintance with Sun. With the passing of years the ties of friendship have increased, and we have learned more than ever to appreciate his strength of character, his earnestness of purpose, his modesty of mind, and to understand the secret of his power, whereby he was enabled to bring to a successful issue the great work of his life.

My chief regret is that I have been able to paint so meagre a picture of a truly noble character.

JAMES CANTLIE.

CONTENTS

FIRST STAMP OF THE REPUBLIC OF CHINA,
BEARING THE HEAD OF SUN YAT SEN.

DOLLAR OF THE REPUBLIC OF CHINA, SHOW-
ING THE HEAD OF SUN YAT SEN AND
ON THE REVERSE THE INSCRIPTION IN
ENGLISH.

I

INTRODUCTORY

IT was in the autumn of 1896 that the world first heard of Dr. Sun Yat Sen. A Chinese refugee had been kidnapped—kidnapped in London; and Englishmen rubbed their eyes as they read how he had been seized in broad daylight, and was being held a prisoner in the Chinese Embassy, his liberty denied him, his very life in danger. Who does not remember the sensation the story caused, the tense excitement as to the man's fate, the wild conjectures as to the mode of his delivery? For a day or so the town, the whole country, talked of little else. And then, suddenly, Britain intervened! Within a few days Sun was released. Almost as speedily, for the excitement soon subsided, he was forgotten.

But a decade and a half later the public recalled the strange event. For, on December 29, 1911, they read with something like amazement the message from Reuter's Nanking correspondent telling the world that this same refugee, who had been hunted out of his own land and pursued even in ours, had lived to be proclaimed First President of the Chinese Republic and, quite obviously, was master of the unprecedented situation which had been created in that land of mystery. What had happened in the interval to give him this unique authority? How had this man, poor, obscure, unaided, achieved so wonderful a sway over the countless millions of his fellow-Celestials, usually deemed the most elusive of mankind? In what lay the secret of his power? To answer these questions, so that the public may see Sun Yat Sen and the Chinese Revolution in their true perspective, is to describe a career that, alike for sheer romance and historical importance, has never been surpassed.

For twenty years Sun Yat Sen has devoted every day and almost every hour of his life to one single object—the overthrow of the Manchu rule in China and the establishment of such representative Government as will insure the people elementary justice, freedom from the extortions of corrupt mandarins, a free press, and facilities for education. He has risked death and torture on innumerable occasions. He has travelled on foot throughout a large part of the four million square miles of China, and, under various disguises, he has penetrated to almost every nook of his native country and left representatives in almost every town, building up, with matchless skill and patience, an organization whose network has gradually spread over the whole of that vast Empire.

More, he has drawn upon the huge reserve of Chinese scattered in thousands all over the world, and to his countrymen in America, Honolulu, Japan, the Malay Peninsula and the Straits Settlements he has carried the message of revolt against the Manchu dynasty—the dynasty that every Chinese hates instinctively. He has visited these exiles repeatedly, gaining with each visit some new recruit or gleaning information that made possible some further avenue of activity inside the Flowery Land. He has bought arms in Europe to smuggle them through under the very nose of the authorities. He has made friends at many European Embassies, and—hardest task of all— he has induced the Powers, through their representatives, to hold their hands whilst China worked out her own salvation.

All this he has done, aided at first by only a few devoted friends, without resources of his own, and with his life and safety perpetually menaced by the ubiquitous Manchu agents, who have left no stone unturned to destroy him or his influence.

That he has succeeded so far as to bring China within sight of deliverance stamps him as one of the most remarkable men of our time. We have only to reflect for a moment upon the magnitude of his task, to recall the almost overwhelming obstacles confronting him, to realize how great a part he has played in the world's history.

For if ever there was a country that offered difficulties to the organizing of a revolution, that surely was China. First, there is the almost overwhelming magnitude of the territory. To say that China has an area of 4,218,201 square miles is only to confuse the mind. But when we remember that the Empire is one-third larger than all Europe, that it is bigger than the United States, with Alaska and Great Britain thrown in (it is, in fact, a fourth of the habitable globe), we get some idea of its immensity. To arrange for men to act in concert over an area so great as this, or any large portion of it, is to overcome a difficulty that seems almost insuperable. Then consider the temperament of the people. They have been described as " moving less in centuries than Western people do in decades." " For nearly five thousand years," says Dr. Arthur

J. Brown in his book, " New Forces in Old China," " they have lived apart, sufficient unto themselves, cherishing their own ideals, plodding along their well-worn paths, ignorant of or indifferent to the progress of the Western world, mechanically memorizing dead classics, and standing still comparatively amid the tremendous onrush of modern civilization." The very resources of their own land they have allowed to lie neglected. Baron von Richthofen estimates that they have 419,000 square miles underlaid with coal, of which 600,000,000,000 tons are anthracite, and that the single province of Shen-si could supply the entire world with coal for a thousand years. Add to this, apparently inexhaustible quantities of iron ore, and we have, of course, the two products on which material greatness largely depends. But the coal and iron are both unworked! It is not so very long ago since the Chinese Government acquired the first railway constructed in China. It ran from Shanghai to Wu-sung, and great was the excitement of the populace; but no sooner was it completed than the Government bought it, tore up the road-bed and dumped the engines into the river—*pour encourager les autres!* To-day the great bulk of the population of China are as untouched by railways as they are by

modern thought or literature. "Books on
politics," said Sun Yat Sen, "are not allowed; daily newspapers are prohibited in
China; the world around, its people and
politics, are shut out; while no one below the
rank of a mandarin of the seventh rank is
allowed to read Chinese geography, far less
foreign.

"The laws of the present dynasty are
not for public reading; they are known only
to the highest officials. The reading of books
on military subjects is, in common with that
of other prohibited matter, not only forbidden, but is even punishable by death. No
one is allowed, on pain of death, to invent
anything new, or to make known any new
discovery. In this way are the people kept
in darkness, while the Government doles out
to them what scraps of information it finds
will suit its own ends."

That Government's own decrees are elo-
quent of the benighted condition of the people and of the almost incredible apathy that
has fallen upon them. Take, for instance,
the edict issued by the late Empress Dowager
in November, 1906, in which she complains
that "officials and people are separated by
the employment of forms and ceremonies so
as to make all matters neglected. These
officials do not pay attention to the welfare

or troubles of those under them, and often to such an extent are they indifferent and corrupt that relatives and secretaries are permitted to browbeat and oppress the masses, while the gate-keepers and runners of the Yamens prey upon and devour the substance of the people. In such circumstances can any one expect these local governments to flourish? How can the spirits of the people, moreover, be elevated under such a state of affairs? Dwelling upon this point makes us feel very indignant indeed." Can we imagine such a confession of impotency being addressed to a European people without exciting the promptest and most stimulating of replies? But the Chinese grins and bears it, or rather he did until a few months ago.

The fact is that long ago there descended upon him the paralyzing blight of spiritual pride, and until very recent days its fetters have hung heavily on his soul. When the rest of the world was sunk in barbarism, China had a great, a splendid civilization of her own. Her people had created great buildings while Europeans had no better shelter than caves, her astronomers made accurate observations two hundred years before Abraham left Ur. "They used firearms," says Dr. Brown, "at the beginning

of the Christian era; they first grew tea,
manufactured gunpowder, made pottery,
glue, and gelatine; they invented printing in
movable types five hundred years before that
art was known in Europe; they discovered
the principles of the mariner's compass
without which the oceans could not be
crossed, conceived the idea of artificial water-
ways, and dug a canal six hundred miles
long; they made mountain roads which, in
the opinion of Dr. S. Wells Williams, ' when
new, probably equalled in engineering and
construction anything of the kind ever built
by the Romans '; and they invented the
arch to which our modern architecture is so
greatly indebted.''

It is not surprising, therefore, that with
triumphs and achievements such as these
to their credit, and with no rival, no com-
petitor in civilization, near their throne, the
Chinese became wedded to the idea that other
nations were negligible quantities, barbarians who did not count, that they alone were
the people, and wisdom would die with them.
The obsession has remained nearly to our
own day, and when Lord Napier proceeded
to Canton, empowered by an Act of Parliament to negotiate with the Chinese regarding trade '' to and from the dominions of the
Emperor of China, and for the purpose of

protecting and promoting such trade," the
Governor of Canton explained that he could
not possibly receive a letter from the said
barbarian, *i.e.,* Lord Napier. Said he:
" There has never been such a thing as outside barbarians sending a letter. . . . It is
contrary to everything of dignity and de-
corum. The thing is most decidedly impossible. . . . The barbarians of this nation
(Great Britain) coming or leaving Canton
have, beyond their trade, not any public
business; and the commissioned officers of
the Celestial Empire never take cognizance
of the trivial affairs of trade. . . . The some
hundreds of thousands of commercial duties
yearly coming from the said nation concern
not the Celestial Empire to the extent of a
hair or a feather's down. The possession
or absence of them is utterly unworthy of
one careful thought."

It is this temper of mind that any one
bent on creating a revolution in China
would find himself most emphatically " up
against "—an insular complacency that re-
fuses even to consider outside events, and
accepts its own surroundings as quite " the
best in the best of all possible worlds."
Can one imagine a greater obstacle to any
projected reform, based necessarily upon the
experience of other nations?

Yet one such obstacle confronted Sun Yat Sen. Greater than China's immensity, greater even than the apathy which has fallen upon her citizens, was the hideous, ceaseless pressure of the Manchu tyranny. Nothing quite like it has ever before been known. In the days of European autocracy, the power of the Crown was always liable to effective challenge, first by the nobles, later by Parliament. But in China there is no Parliament and all the nobles are Manchus, jealous of their special prerogatives and all despising the Chinese, while every officer of state, from the governor of a province down to a policeman, is in favor, and for very obvious reasons, of maintaining the despotism at its height. Why is this? Again to quote from Sun Yat Sen: "English readers are probably unaware of the smallness of the established salaries of provincial magnates. They will scarcely credit that the Viceroy of, say, Canton, ruling a country with a population larger than that of Great Britain, is allowed as his legal salary the paltry sum of £60 a year; so that, in order to live and maintain himself in office, accumulating fabulous riches the while, he resorts to extortion and the selling of justice. So-called education and the results of examinations are the one means of obtain-

THE GREAT WALL AT NANKOW PASS

ing official notice. Granted that a young scholar gains distinction, he proceeds to seek public employment, and, by bribing the Peking authorities, an official post is hoped for. Once obtained, as he cannot live on his salary, perhaps he even pays so much annually for his post, license to squeeze is the result, and the man must be stupid indeed who cannot, when backed up by Government, make himself rich enough to buy a still higher post in a few years. With advancement comes increased license and additional facility for self-enrichment, so that the cleverest ' squeezer ' ultimately can obtain money enough to purchase the highest positions.[1]

" This official thief, with his mind warped by his mode of life, is the ultimate authority in all matters of social, political, and criminal life. It is a feudal system, an *imperium in imperio,* an unjust autocracy, which thrives by its own rottenness. But this system of fattening on the public vitals—the

[1] See how this system worked out as regards the individual Chinese. An English lady, resident near Canton, had for many years an excellent servant in her employ—veracious and reliable. He applied for leave of absence to inspect some coal-mines in which his savings had been invested. He would be absent only a few days, he said. Alas ! he was absent some months, and returned an emaciated wreck. He had been seized by a mandarin—imprisoned, beaten, tortured, and made to surrender his shares in the mines.

selling of power—is the chief means by which the Manchu dynasty continues to exist. With this legalized corruption stamped as the highest ideal of government, who can wonder at the strong undercurrent of dissatisfaction among the people? "

Thus has the Manchu dynasty been maintained! It may be said, even so, was it not still open to wise and patriotic Chinese to make some organized effort to instruct the people?

That is a question natural for any Westerner to ask. To a Chinese it appears too extravagant to answer, because there is an obstacle to the execution of such a project, which would be present to his mind the moment it was proposed.

At first blush there is something wildly incredible about the idea of a single clan able to exercise espionage over an entire empire, and that empire the vastest in the world. But what are the facts? The Manchus have only kept their hold upon China by a system of terrorism and spying. The eye of the Emperor is everywhere—in the most humble cottage of the most remote village; in the crowded workroom; at the factory gate; in the railway carriage; at the domestic fireside; everywhere! China has been honeycombed by an army of spies—

spies who report a word, a hint of sedition, who act silently and swiftly, and whose superiors strike ruthlessly; spies who betray the confidences of relatives, the secrets of friends, who are without compunction, whose very identity is unsuspected and from whose inquisition nothing is hidden. Let a stranger come to a village in China, and within a few hours the authorities are informed; let a man whisper treason, and his life is forfeit. The very interior of the palace itself is infested with agents and eunuchs whose ears are strained to catch the faintest whisper of the hated word " reform," and who spy even upon the secret councils of their master, so that when, twelve years ago, Kuang Hsü, the reforming Emperor, dared to contemplate some mitigation of the Manchu prerogatives, he was seized, conveyed a prisoner to an island palace, and " relegated to the nothingness of harem life."

But where the Emperor failed, Sun Yat Sen succeeded. He has triumphed over three obstacles to revolution that seemed insuperable. First, an empire chaotic and immense; secondly, a people steeped in contemptuous ignorance; lastly, a despotism that stood armed at all points between the people and every avenue of knowledge. Let us see how he contrived to overcome them.

II

SUN YAT SEN: THE MAN AND HIS WORK

IN 1894 Dr. Sun Yat Sen joined a society in Canton of some eighteen prominent members whose object was the mending or ending of the Manchu monarchical power. In 1912 this great work was accomplished. Of the eighteen members seventeen were beheaded shortly after the inception of the idea, and Sun was the only member of the original " conspirators " left to carry on the great upheaval. On February 12, 1912, the Manchu Emperor abdicated and Sun Yat Sen's purpose and life-work was accomplished. Others have helped him, others have granted him sympathy and advice, others have given freely of their substance to carry on the work, but as the inceptor, the organizer, and the focus of all this great work Sun Yat Sen stands alone. History will assign him his proper place, but to the onlooker of to-day it is difficult to anticipate fully the tribute of credit which will be his.

SUN YAT SEN AND HIS SON IN 1911

The modern world professes to dislike heroes and heroics; everything tends to " strangle heroes " in these later times, and Sun Yat Sen would have been strangled in fact on many occasions had not a power which may well be termed supernatural preserved him through storm and strife to accomplish his destiny. Not only did his own countrymen set a price on his head and make many attempts to silence him for ever; not only have the official foreign representatives in Peking held his name and his aims in contempt, passing him by with contumely as but a loud-tongued demagogue, but certain important newspapers, even when the whole world hung on his decisions concerning China's future, hesitated to print his very name, or to refer to his being, hoping thereby no doubt to minimize his influence and if possible to obliterate his power. What could this man, born of humble parents in an out-of-the-way Chinese village, know of sovereigns, of principalities, and powers? What could he do to upset an established dynasty and to uproot an ancient form of government which had held sway in China for centuries and controlled the destinies of some 400,000,000 people?

He was declared to have neither influence, money, nor the training considered neces-

sary to organize a revolt, the magnitude of
which has never been surpassed. He was at
best a poor doctor who by a struggle gathered sufficient money together to keep him
alive whilst yet he learned the rudiments of
science and acquired a knowledge of medicine. A poor training, it would seem, for his
life's work, but one which helped him to attain his ends and to bring salvation to his
fellow-countrymen. Sun, however, had a
greater power than either position, money or
education could give him.

Though deep-seated discontent simmered
in the land, it seemed impossible to develop
a master-mind in China fitted for the great
task of reform from amongst the rich, the
powerful, the families of ancient lineage, or
the philosophic *literati;* so Providence selected a man from the humbler classes, a
man endowed with gifts which money cannot buy, nor all the learning of East or West
produce. What were these gifts? According to Christian doctrines they may be
summed in the words, Faith, Hope, and
Charity—a firm faith in the belief that was
within him; hope for the speedy regeneration of China, and charity towards neighbors.
Charity in the true sense of the word is
Sun's outstanding characteristic. An unkind
thought, far less an unkind word, is foreign

to his nature; a keen regard for the feelings of those around him is apparent in his every word and deed; unselfishness to a degree undreamt of amongst modern men; a living expression of the Sermon on the Mount. Such are some of the gifts of this extraordinary man; gifts which command success, which bind his friends to him with "hoops of steel," and have, not only amongst his countrymen, but also amongst the few Europeans and Americans who know Sun Yat Sen as he is, found men willing to devote their energies, their time, their very lives to forward his aims, not alone for the cause he has at heart, but also for the man himself. The secret of his success is unselfishness—seeking only his country's good, not his own advancement; a patriot indeed with no axe to grind, no place seeker, willing to rule if called upon, ready and anxious to stand aside when the interests of his country are to be benefited thereby.

Why was he listened to by his astute countrymen, when all others had failed in regenerating China? Why? The transparent honesty of the man; his manifest patriotism; the simplicity of his character; the readiness to endure all for his country's sake, even torture and death. Persecuted, imprisoned, slighted, a price set on his head, stamped as an outcast and turned out of home and country, refused shelter now by one nation, now by another, until the wide world seemed to afford no place of safety where he could find rest. Neither in fact nor in fiction, neither in history nor in the ideals of romance has any author dared to endow the heroes of his creation with persecutions such as his; for under no flag was he safe; nor in the uttermost parts of the earth, for a period of well-nigh twenty years, could he feel that a cruel death was not imminent.

The idea of getting rid of the Manchus was no modern idea in China. A powerful and widespread body, "The Triad Society," had existed almost ever since the Manchus ascended the throne, but it consisted of men of philosophic ideas without the capability or courage to put their ideas into practice. It was not until Sun Yat Sen came to the front that the idea was given concrete shape and brought to practical issue; the old Triad Society, however, gave little direct help during the recent crisis, the members being afraid of action, for they well knew what failure meant. In China the death penalty was ever at hand when reforms were even whispered, and it was only when Sun took his life in his hand and boldly declared his intentions that any one was found courageous enough to denounce the Throne openly.

Sun Yat Sen was born in 1867 in the province of Kwang-tung, in a remote village situated between the city of Canton and the Portuguese colony of Macao, some thirty miles south of Hong Kong. His father was a convert to Christianity, and was employed as a missionary agent by the London Missionary Society. An English lady connected with the mission interested herself in the young lad, and by her help Sun was well grounded in English. At the age of eighteen Sun became attached to the hospital of the Anglo-American Mission in Canton, then under the direction of a surgeon of considerable repute, Dr. Kerr. He became deeply interested in medicine and surgery, and when twenty years of age he came to Hong Kong to prosecute his studies in the newly.opened College of Medicine.

It was in Hong Kong in 1887 I first met Sun Yat Sen; he came as a student to the College of Medicine for Chinese established in October of that year. I conceived the idea of establishing a college of the kind on my way out to China, and from the time I landed there in June, 1887, until October of that year I followed up the idea and found ready help from Dr. (now Sir) Patrick Manson,

Dr. Wm. Hartigan, Dr. Jordan, Mr. (now Sir) James Stewart Lockhart, Governor of Wei-hai-wei, and perhaps most important of all, Ho Kai (now Sir Ho Kai), M.D., Aberdeen, and barrister-at-law. Ho Kai, in loving memory of his wife, Alice, an English lady, founded a hospital in Hong Kong, under the auspices of the London Missionary Society, and styled it the " Alice Memorial Hospital." There the College of Medicine held its classes, and within its walls the students were given instruction in practical medicine and surgery. The college flourished largely owing to the exertions of Dr. J. C. Thomson, and several of the medical and scientific men in Hong Kong have devotedly continued the work without payment or reward of any kind. The College of Medicine is now merged in the University of Hong Kong, and what should be, and what will become, if properly supported, the nucleus of the greatest centre of Western teaching for China, was thus brought unpretentiously, but none the less effectively, into being.

After five years' study Sun obtained the diploma to practise medicine and surgery from the College of Medicine. He was the first graduate of the College; and shortly afterwards he commenced to practise his profession in the Portuguese colony of

Macao. He was tempted thither from the fact that Macao was adjacent to the village in which he was born, and because he had many friends in the district. In a large, well-built hospital Chinese patients were treated according to native methods. Sun impressed upon the Chinese governors of the hospital the importance and benefits of Western medicine; the future emancipator of China commended himself to these old-world-bred men by his honesty and unselfishness, as he did later to the whole mass of his countrymen. He persuaded them to open the portals of the hospital to admit him with his newly acquired knowledge. With a largeness of mind characteristic of the Chinese the governors said, " Certainly, we will devote this wing of the hospital to European methods, and the other to Chinese practice, and we will judge the results." Is there another people in the world who would have answered thus? I doubt it. It was the action of large-minded, broad-viewed, high-principled, unprejudiced men; an action characteristic, to those who know the Chinese, a people endowed with lofty ideas and willing to act upon them when thoroughly convinced of their possible benefits.

The Chinese are ready students, earnest in their endeavor, quick to understand, retentive of memory. It was perhaps the last-named feature that astonished one most. In Chinese schools everything is given over to training the memory. Knowledge, as we understand it, is quite a secondary factor in the so-called education given in Chinese schools. Moreover, no real instruction is permitted to be given to the people according to Manchu laws. Repetition, unceasing repetition, is the essence of school-life in China. The mind is stored with words and sounds often wholly unintelligible to the scholar nor understood by the teacher. The effect of this constant repetition and memorizing is to develop a retentiveness of memory to a degree unbelievable to those who have not come into contact with Oriental students. A good example of the surprising extent to which memory can be cultivated occurred at one of the professional examinations for the diploma of the College of Medicine. The questions were answered perfectly, but on comparing the papers it was found that the answers were identical. Paragraphs, sentences, full stops, and commas were so placed that it did not matter which of the papers was looked at. The wording was the same. The examiners, new to Chinese methods of instruction, insisted on another paper being set, as they believed the students had by some means copied from each other. A fresh paper of five questions was set, and a careful watch kept during the examination. Again the answers were correct and identical in every point, and it was only when the text-book recommended to the class was referred to that an explanation was forthcoming. They knew the large text-book of some five hundred pages by heart, and could answer any question put them word for word from the book.

Sun commenced practice, and I encouraged him especially in surgical work. When major operations had to be done I went on several occasions to Macao to assist him, and there, in the presence of the governors of the hospital, he performed important operations, requiring skill, coolness of judgment, and dexterity. It was a goodly journey to Macao by sea, and took me away a considerable time from my daily routine of work. Why did I go this journey to Macao to help this man? For the reason that others have fought for and died for him, because I loved and respected him. His is a nature that draws men's regard towards him and makes them ready to serve him at the operating-table or on the battlefield; an unexplainable influence, a magnetism which prevails and finds its expression in attracting men to his side.

Surgical work is not conducted in China with the privacy that attends similar work with us. At Sun's operations the lay committee of the hospital came and seated themselves near the operating-table, and the relatives and friends of the patient stood around watching the proceedings attentively. Especially did the manipulations in cutting for stone interest the onlookers. It was an operation that appealed to most men in that part of the country, for stone was not an uncommon ailment in the neighborhood. The necessary incisions to reach the stone required a good deal of " fanning " on the part of the onlookers to keep them from fainting —every man carries a fan in the south of China; but when the stone was produced their qualms were forgotten, and the rejoicings and " Hi-yas " of astonishment showed they were amply rewarded for the trying ordeal they had gone through.

There is much publicity in illness in China, and the doctor's attendance is often made almost a public function. A foreign doctor's visit is of great interest, especially in the country districts and villages. He is followed by all and sundry to the house, and amongst a group of friends around the patient, with the villagers peering round the doorway and occupying every point of vantage, he has to proceed to diagnose the nature of the illness or treat a surgical defect.

That the Chinese medical students are no mere bookworms, as their examination papers would appear to show, but endowed with a practical sense of their duties was brought to light when plague broke out in Hong Kong in 1894. For work in the plague hospital under the control of the Alice Memorial Hospital, with which the College of Medicine was affiliated, the students readily and spontaneously volunteered for duty in the wards. This may seem a small matter to-day, but in 1894 epidemic plague was an unknown disease for some two hundred years in either China or Europe, and the only accurate account of its ravages was gathered from descriptions of the Great Plague of London in the seventeenth century, when exposure to infection meant death.

Yet with the terrors of the disease before them, when many of their friends and relations were dead or dying of the disease, and the population fleeing from the plague-stricken city, these students took up their duties in the wards, as clerks, dressers, and even nurses—wards in which every patient attacked died. A more noble example of faithfulness to their profession and heroic devotion has never been recorded. Prowess on

the battlefield, fighting in the stir of strife,
is one thing, but to fact death in a plague
hospital, or a cholera camp, when all around
are dying, and to continue calmly at work
day after day, night after night, and week
after week, requires courage of another order. Gordon may have been proud of the
valor of his Chinese troops, but those of us
who saw the work the Chinese students did
during that epidemic of plague are willing to
bestow upon them a higher meed of praise
than ever was acclaimed to the soldiers of
Genghis Khan, before whose very name the
continents of Asia and Europe trembled.
The work of these students shows that China
has men within its fold capable of the highest courage and devotion to duty.

One of the first diversions which I instituted for the students from hospital work
and lectures was the formation of a military
ambulance company. After getting the students proficient in " first aid " and ambulance drill and providing a suitable uniform,
I offered my company to the commandant of
the Hong Kong Volunteer Artillery. The
offer was accepted, and for years the Chinese
students acted as the Ambulance Department
of the Corps. I had just given up the command of the Volunteer Medical Staff Corps,
now the R.A.M.C. (T.F.), in London, and

found that the Chinese students compared quite favorably with the London medical students in their aptitude and efficiency. I also induced the students to play cricket, and several of them, Sun included, gave promise of becoming good all-round cricketers, an accomplishment which in English eyes will at once commend the young men to favorable consideration.

In Macao, Sun first heard of " The Young China Party," a legend we have become familiar with in relation to the " Young Turkish Party." Had there been a Sun Yat Sen in Turkey the revolution of that party would have been a success; there are in Turkey revolutionists in plenty, but few true patriots, otherwise she would now be on the high road to success and liberty. Sun, however, had to quit Macao, because, under Portuguese regulations, no one not possessing a Portuguese diploma could legitimately practise there, and so he removed to Canton to work. The activities, however, of the reform party became so pronounced, and Sun became so prominent amongst his colleagues, that he found little time for any work except political. How the attempt to capture Canton and its arsenal failed is told later on; how of all the prominent reformers Sun was the only one to escape alive is well known.

With Sun's many escapes my wife and myself have been made, from time to time, fully
acquainted, but it was not my intention to
relate them until given permission to do so
by Sun himself. In the *Strand Magazine,*
April, 1912, Sun gives an account of several
of these. His first escape was soon after he
came to Canton after giving up his practice
in Macao. He had enrolled himself as a member of the Young China Party, and in 1894
formed a branch of the Kao-lao-hui in Canton. Knowing that the Emperor Kuang
Hsü had serious intentions of introducing reforms in governmental methods, Sun forwarded a petition signed by many of his
adherents to the Emperor. All was quiet
until the war with Japan was settled, when
the imperious Dowager-Empress reassumed
the direction of affairs and denounced the
intentions of the Emperor and all reformers.
With the cessation of hostilities against
Japan, a number of the disbanded soldiers
in Canton became riotous owing to want of
pay and employment. The Canton police at
the same time, owing to their pay not being
forthcoming, took to looting the shops in the
city. A meeting of indignant citizens was
held, an unheard-of proceeding, and a depu-
tation five hundred strong presented themselves at the house of the Governor of the

city. After hearing their demands the Governor regarded their presumption in the light of a rebellion and arrested the ringleaders. Sun had the good fortune to escape, but determined forthwith to rescue his companions who had been seized. That was his first escape.

His second was more precarious. In the city of Swatow, some hundred and fifty miles north of Canton, something like a rebellion had prevailed for some time. Sun and his colleagues approached the revolutionaries and found them willing to join forces with him. The bold plan was then formed of seizing the city of Canton as the only means whereby they could get what they considered their just claims conceded. Rifles, pistols, ammunition, and even dynamite were collected from every possible source, and a recruiting agent was sent to Hong Kong to enlist men and to purchase arms.

The plot so far succeeded, but when all seemed ready news came from Swatow that the men could not move, as information concerning the rising had leaked out and the Government had the Tartar garrisons under arms and ready for action. Without the Swatow force nothing could be accomplished; and telegrams were sent to Hong Kong to stop the sailing of the contingent. The men, some four hundred strong, were on the quay at Hong Kong ready to go aboard the steamer for Canton. Several barrels containing pistols had been already shipped when the officer in charge of the contingent received a telegram telling him not to proceed to Canton and to disband the men. The officer, however, unfortunately misread the telegram and allowed the men to embark, with the result that they were captured in a body on reaching Canton. Thereupon, the Central Reform Committee broke up their headquarters in Canton, burnt their papers, hid their arms, and escaped from the city as best they could.

Sun gained a friend's house; at night he was let down over the city wall and sought refuge on the canal banks to the south of the city. Here he wandered on towards home, now travelling in canal boats, now seeking the shore when soldiers came to search the boats for refugees, and finally reaching Macao, where he was hidden by friends. Macao, however, became too dangerous, and he went from thence to Hong Kong, then to Kobé and from there to Honolulu.

It was not until fully a year after the Canton affair, when on my way home from China, via Honolulu across America, that I knew of his whereabouts. The vehicle in which I was driving with my wife, and a Japanese nurse in charge of my son, through the streets of Honolulu was stopped by a man, apparently a Japanese, looking very trim in European dress and with a moustache of respectable dimensions, who proffered his hand, raised his hat, and smiled affably. We all regarded him with astonishment; the Japanese nurse addressed him in Japanese, but he shook his head in response, and it was some time before we recognized it was Sun minus his cue and Chinese dress. A cordial greeting ensued and a visit to us in London was arranged.

The resemblance of the Chinese to his Japanese neighbor when he is " got-up " in the same way is most marked; so identical do the two appear, that when we visited a shop in Honolulu the shopman addressed Sun, who was with us, in Japanese, and would not believe his repeated statement that he was not Japanese, but Chinese. Should the Chinese follow the example of the Japanese and lay aside their national dress, the identity of each will possibly disappear, and even the two peoples will not be able to recognize by their appearance to which nationality they belong. A pity in many ways, yet evidently an inevitable result of the modernizing of both China and Japan.

Sun gives the following account of his experiences, about this time; he says:

" At Hong Kong my safety was hardly more assured, and on Dr. Cantlie's advice I went to see a lawyer, Mr. Dennis, who told me that my best protection was instant flight.

" ' Peking's arm, though weaker, is still a long one,' he said, ' and in whichever part of the world you go, you must expect to hear of the Tsung-li-Yamen.'

" Fortunately, friends provided me with funds, and here I must mention the constant fidelity of well-wishers to the great cause I have all these years endeavored to promote. They have never failed me. But then, fortunately, apart from travelling, my wants are few. I have often for weeks together lived on a little rice and water, and I have journeyed many hundreds of miles on foot. At other times I have had difficulty in refusing the large sums placed at my disposal, for some of my countrymen in America are very rich, generous, and patriotic.

" At Kobé, whither I fled from Hong Kong, I took a step of great importance. I cut off my cue, which had been growing all my life. For some days I had not shaved my head, and I allowed the hair to grow on my upper lip. Then I went out to a clothier's and bought a suit of modern Japanese garments. When I was fully dressed I looked in the mirror, and was astonished—and a good deal reassured—by the transformation. Nature had favored me. I was darker in complexion than most Chinese, a trait I had inherited from my mother, for my father resembled more the regular type. I have seen it said that I have Malay blood in my veins, and also that I was born in Honolulu. Both these statements are false. I am purely Chinese, as far as I know; but after the Japanese War, when the natives of Japan began to be treated with more respect, I had no trouble, when I had let my hair and moustache grow, in passing for a Japanese. I admit I owe a great deal to this circumstance, as otherwise I should not have escaped from many dangerous situations.

" A similar experience befell me in Honolulu, where I spent six months after leaving Japan. I found many of my countrymen there, and they received me with open arms. They knew all about my exploits, and they also knew that a big price was placed on the head of the notorious ' Sun Wen.' In the town of Honolulu I held a sort of *levée* every day, and I received letters and reports from my friends, the members of the Reform Party, the Kao-lao-hui. Thence I went to San Francisco, and enjoyed a sort of triumphal journey through America, varied by reports that the Chinese Minister to Washington was doing his utmost to have me kidnapped and carried back to China, where I well knew the fate that would befall me—first having my ankles crushed in a vice and broken by a hammer, my eyelids cut off, and, finally, be chopped to small fragments, so that none could claim my mortal remains. For the old Chinese code does not err on the side of mercy to political agitators.

" I sailed for England in September, 1896, and
on the eleventh of the next month I was kidnapped
at the Chinese Legation in Portland Place, London, by order of the Chinese Ambassador. The
story of that kidnapping is already known fully to
the world. It is enough to say here that I was
locked up in a room under strict surveillance for
twelve days, awaiting my transportation on board
ship, as a lunatic, back to China, and that I should
never have escaped had not my old friend and
master, Dr. Cantlie, been then living in London.
To him I managed, after many failures, to get
through a message. He notified the newspapers,
and the police and Lord Salisbury intervened at
the eleventh hour and ordered my release."

Many inquiries have been sent to me,
" How did you get information that Sun was
imprisoned in the Legation? " As usual, a
woman came to the rescue. The wife of one
of the English servants in the Legation heard
from her husband of the piteous plight of
the imprisoned Chinese and sent me the following letter. " There is a friend of yours
imprisoned in the Chinese Legation here
since last Sunday; they intend sending him
out to China, where it is certain they will
hang him. It is very sad for the poor man,
and unless something is done at once he will
be taken away and no one will know it. I
dare not sign my name, but this is the truth,
so believe what I say. Whatever you do

must be done at once, or it will be too late. His name is, I believe, Sin Yin Sen." The note reached my house at 11:30 P.M. on the night of Saturday, October 17, 1896. A ring at the door-bell brought me from my bed. I found no one at the door, but observed and picked up the letter, which had been pushed in below the door. It was this woman who started the machinery for Sun's release. Had this humble woman failed in her purpose the regeneration of China would have been thrown back indefinitely, for the last of the reformers would have lost his life and the Manchus would be still in power.

I went to the head of the Marylebone police and thence to Scotland Yard the moment I received the information of his whereabouts. The chief difficulty was to get any one to believe the story. The police even at Scotland Yard said it was none of their business, and that I had done my duty when I reported the matter to them, and that I ought to go home and keep quiet. My visit was at 1.30 A.M., and they told me the next day, when I called with Sir Patrick Manson, that a man had called in the middle of the night with the same statement, and that the inspector on duty could not make out whether he was drunk or a lunatic. I told the inspector now on duty I was the same man, and again he gave me the advice to go home and keep quiet and that they could do nothing in the matter as it did not concern them. When asked to whom I should report the matter, I was told I had done my duty by reporting the matter to them, and that was enough.

The want of initiative amongst the men " on duty " at Scotland Yard it is needless to comment upon. Had I got in touch with those in higher authority the matter might have been different; but it taught me the lesson so often preached, namely, that the difference between the " classes " of men is the presence or absence of initiative. It was not until I got in touch with a member of the clerical staff at the Foreign Office, quite at the eleventh hour, that the matter was taken up and dealt with. Had I not been fortunate enough to meet a man accustomed to take initiative, " the dangerous lunatic " at the Chinese Legation would, twenty-four hours later, have been shipped to China to be punished in the way all Sun's colleagues had already been—namely, by decapitation. Emissaries of the Chinese Government haunted Sun's footsteps in Japan, in China, in Annam, and wherever he went. The enormous price set upon his head induced desperate men readily to undertake either his capture or his death.

Of his experiences after the kidnapping episode Sun writes:

" After some time spent in travel and study in London and Paris, I felt that the time had come to return to China. My country, I felt, needed me, and I arrived to find everything in a state of ferment. The whole world knows the story of the Boxer troubles. During that terrible time I was speaking and writing and lecturing—more confident now than ever that nothing could stave off the inevitable revolution. Daily I carried my life in my hand, for I began to have enemies now amongst the extremists, men who hated Europeans and European civilization, and wished to expel the ' foreign devils ' from China.

" It was now that another important event happened to me. I was speaking to a company of my followers, when my eye fell on a young man of slight physique. He was under five feet high; he was about my age; his face was pale, and he looked delicate. Afterwards he came to me and said:

" ' I should like to throw in my lot with you. I should like to help you. I believe your propaganda will succeed.'

" His accent told me he was an American. He held out his hand. I took it and thanked him, wondering who he was. I thought he was a missionary or a student. I was right. After he had gone I said to a friend:

" ' Who was that little hunchback? '

" ' Oh, that,' said he, ' is Colonel Homer Lea,

one of the most brilliant—perhaps *the* most brilliant military genius now alive. He is a perfect master of modern warfare.'

" I almost gasped in astonishment.

" ' And he has just offered to throw in his lot with me.'

" The next morning I called on Homer Lea, now General, and the famous author of the ' Valor of Ignorance.' I told him that in case I should succeed and my countrymen gave me the power to do so, I would make him my chief military adviser.

" ' Do not wait until you are President of China,' he said. ' You may want me before then. You can neither make nor keep a Government without an army. I have the highest opinion of Chinamen as troops when they are properly trained.'

" Most of the modern army—the troops trained in European tactics—are patriots and reformers, but until they seized the arsenal at Hanyang they were without ammunition. Blank cartridges were all that was ever served out to them.''

After his release from the Chinese Embassy in London in October, 1896, Sun stayed with us for some time before leaving for the Far East. His narrow escape did not check his intentions, but sent him forth more fully determined than ever to achieve his purpose. In Japan he found asylum, and from there he trav-

elled incognito in various disguises which I
even now do not feel justified in disclosing.
He visited many parts of the interior of
China, the Straits Settlements, the Malay
Peninsula, the United States, and wherever
Chinese had emigrated he preached reform
and the necessity for strenuous endeavor.
What did he preach? A bloodless reform,
a reform by peaceful measures; convincing
arguments were his weapons. The foe he set
out to crush was the prevailing apathy and
the political ignorance of his countrymen and
their terror of declaring their real feelings.
To raise troops of soldiers from amongst the
floating population of China ready to fight for
pay and to drive the Manchus from Peking
would have been a light task compared to
the work Sun set himself to do. He resolved
that the *people* of China should " rebel " in
the true sense of the word; but how was this
to be done? As Sun did it.

In the interior of China, in a guise which
defied the penetration of the officials, he
preached the tenets of his belief. To the
villagers on the banks of the mighty Yang-
tse he brought tidings of liberty from its
mouth in the China Seas to far Sze-chuen on
the borders of Thibet; on the Pearl River
he drew crowds to listen to him, and throughout the Kwangsi and Kwang-tung provinces

established centres of influence and gained able and enthusiastic supporters as his adherents. As a spectacled pedlar with knickknacks in his wallet he travelled through the Malay Peninsula and the Straits Settlements, attracting not only the laboring coolies in the plantations but the masters as well. The well-to-do merchants in Penang and Singapore gave him their support and contributed sums of money to further the campaign he had in hand. In Honolulu, in San Francisco and other cities and centres of the United States, Sun converted men to his standard and gained their confidence by his convincing honesty and unselfish patriotism. A simple talent apparently, but one that has served to bring light and hope to human beings before now, has stirred men to the highest efforts and founded the greatest of all the religions of the world.

How did he preach? Was Sun the blatant, loud-tongued demagogue his European detractors would have us believe? Far other were the measures he adopted. In a recently published article, a well-known author gives an account of an address he heard delivered by Sun to a large meeting of Chinese in San Francisco. For three hours did he speak, quietly, seriously, without once pitching his tones in passionate appeal or ever raising his hand to enforce his arguments. A simple sermon, during which his hearers neither applauded nor gave sign of dissent— a spellbound audience listening to a message which had been denied them for centuries. A message of hope to escape from a thraldom compared with which the monarchical and religious tyranny of the Middle Ages in Western Europe appears as comparative freedom, for in China the people have no say whatever in the management of Imperial, national, or even municipal affairs; the mandarins or local magistrates have full power of adjudication, from which there is no appeal. Their word is law, and they have full scope to practise their machinations with complete irresponsibility, and to fatten on the people with impunity. Extortion by officials is a recognized institution, the means by which the official lives and thrives. Appointments are procured by bribery, and once obtained the holder has complete license, and the higher the position he acquires the greater additional facilities are afforded for aggrandizement and self-enrichment; these officers are the ultimate authority in all matters affecting social, political and criminal life.

The so-called education of the masses underwent a change when the Manchus came to rule the country; these uneducated, rude, and

uncultivated people, " outer barbarians," as
the Chinese called them, by a stroke of success in battle found themselves masters of
the situation and seized the throne. Utterly
ignorant of literature of any kind, they found
to their surprise that the Chinese were an
educated people, almost every coolie in the
land could read, write, and count to some
extent, and many were scholars of attainment in the Chinese sense; the Manchus were
alarmed at the state of affairs, and believing
that education was a present danger to them,
they sought to stamp it out. This they found
impossible; so some clever men amongst them
set to work to evolve a system of teaching
which would count for nothing, whilst at the
same time they humored the people by allowing them to prosecute study of a kind. The
writings of Confucius and other sages were
curtailed; all parts relating to the criticism
of their superiors were carefully eliminated,
and only those parts were published for public reading in schools which taught complete
obedience to authority.

To keep the masses in ignorance was the
deliberate purpose of the Manchus; the books
they allowed to be published contained mere
idioms, what we would term " copy-book "
texts. Of instruction these books afforded
none; their reading conveyed no knowledge—

proverbs in poetic language devoid of information, reasoning in a circle which led to
nothing. The boys (for girls were not allowed to be educated) were no better informed when they finished than when they
began. Nothing in history parallels this
sham learning; the people demanded education, and their rulers gave them trite sayings
to read, and kept them in total ignorance.
Sun Yat Sen, in his appeal to his countrymen, had to begin at the very root of reform.

It was not merely a change of dynasty, of
altering or amending laws, nor an extension
of freedom, for none existed. The reform
had to start from complete darkness; not
even from chaos to cosmos, for there were
not present even the very elements which go
to form chaos. There had to be, as it were,
a new heaven and a new earth; a complete
submersion of the past, and a fresh resur-
rection if freedom was to be obtained. No
man ever attempted a task so huge, yet has
it been accomplished by an unpretentious individual with nothing to help him but honesty, unselfishness, ability and a readiness
to lay down his life for his country's sake.

Other escapes from what seemed inevitable
death were many. For safety Sun frequently
lived on board junks on the river as he travelled in the interior of China. Once at Nan-

king a man entered Sun's cabin on board a junk and announced that he had been offered $5,000 to effect his capture. Sun reasoned with the would-be captor, with the result that the man fell at his feet in an agony of repentance and implored pardon. The man desisted. Why? Sun's personality merely, for he was not armed. No one who has come in close touch with Sun Yat Sen but has felt the magic of his presence. Honesty and patriotism endow him with an " atmosphere " that convinces his opponents to his views and serves to turn aside the assassin's knife and the betrayer's purpose. The betrayer in this instance did as another betrayer did, went and hanged himself, as he could not face the world again after having even thought of giving Sun up to his enemies.

Once, when hiding in a fisherman's cabin outside Canton, soldiers were sent to watch the cabin and to shoot Sun at sight; the fisherman got to know of their presence and kept Sun indoors for two days, until, in fact, he was relieved of their attentions by some friend shooting the soldiers themselves.

Once, in the island of Hainan, owing to the house he occupied being watched, he never moved out of the compound for six months, and only by a clever ruse did he manage to get on board a boat and escape.

One of the most serious attempts on his life was made by two young Government officials, attended by a dozen soldiers, in Canton. They entered Sun's room late one evening. The position was desperate, for his capture or death would mean promotion and high rewards to these officers. Even then did Sun's calmness effect his safety. Apprised of their advent, he took up one of the sacred books on the table beside him and read aloud. The would-be captors listened and then began to ask questions. Sun entered into conversation with them, and in two hours' time the officials with their attendant soldiers departed. Sun's personality again told; the officials who came to arrest were themselves arrested by the magnetism of this extraordinary man, who wins all to his cause and sends his captors away happy that they failed in their enterprise.

Thus for some seventeen years—from 1895 to 1912—has death by violence threatened him. More than once has a hired assassin entered the room he occupied; spies have watched him in almost every country, including England and America; a large sum, at one time amounting to $500,000, was offered for his capture, and only now can he be said to be beyond attempts on his life. How did Sun regard these? Latterly with indifference, formerly with some apprehension for the cause he had in hand.

His host in San Francisco told me of his conversation with Sun on this subject. Sun had just spoken to an audience in that city in February, 1911, and when he rose to go his friend proposed accompanying him to his lodging. Sun remonstrated and said there was no occasion for that. His host said that it was very unsafe, seeing that a price was on his head, to go at night through the Chinese quarter of the city. At this Sun smiled, and said that there was no fear. His friend enforced the necessity by saying that it would be the ruin of the cause he had at heart were he to be killed. Whereat Sun again smiled and said, " Oh no, the cause will not be ruined by my death; everything is in order, my death will not affect it, the whole scheme is worked out to the most minute detail; the leaders are appointed, the generals are ready, the troops are organized, and nothing that can happen to me will make any difference. A few years ago, my death would have been a misfortune, but not now.'' Regardless of everything except the welfare of his country, he had no thought of self and refused to be protected. He always spoke in this fashion concerning the dangers he ran. During his many visits to London, although when he left our house he was conscious he was followed, he regarded the matter with indifference.

When he accompanied us to dinner at a friend's house, there was the inevitable spy or detective following us, and when we started to come home we were made aware of being watched and followed. My wife and myself were also "honored" in this fashion on several occasions even when Sun had left the country, and our friends were at times alarmed that we might be punished for our friendship with Sun. Our being followed, however, was no doubt merely due to the fact that Sun had disappeared, and, having lost touch with his whereabouts, the authorities had us shadowed in the hope we were going to visit him at his lodgings, and thereby unwittingly reveal his address.

The early necessity for obtaining the "sinews of war " and his appreciation of his own people Sun has briefly expressed in the following:

" At the close of the Boxer rebellion I returned to America. There was one thing I wanted more than troops and arms—without which I saw I could have neither, and that was money. Not the money in quantities I had been receiving—here and there—but at least half a million sterling. Anything less than this would be failure. Now began a new *rôle* for me—a canvasser for political funds. In this capacity I travelled in every city in America, and I visited all the leading bankers in Europe. Emissaries sent by me penetrated into all quarters. Some professing to act for me and in my name proved faithless. But I prefer not to speak of these—although one man is now universally denounced as a traitor to the cause for having appropriated a huge sum of money entrusted to his care. He will meet with his due reward.

" All over the world, and particularly in America, the legend has grown up that Chinamen are selfish and mercenary. There never was a greater libel on a people. Many have given me their whole fortune. One Philadelphia laundryman called at my hotel after a meeting, and, thrusting a linen bag upon me, went away without a word. It contained his entire savings for twenty years.''

In this sketch of Sun Yat Sen I know how completely I have failed to depict the character of this extraordinary man. My respect and regard for him may appear to have warped my judgment and directed my pen in too narrow a channel. Let there be no mistake in this matter, however; I have restrained, not exaggerated, my feelings towards him. I have never known any one like Sun Yat Sen; if I were asked to name the most perfect character I ever knew, I would unhesitatingly say Sun Yat Sen. In our house he was the most welcome of visitors; children and servants alike conceived a deep regard for him; his sweetness of disposition, his courtesy, his consideration for others, his interesting conversation, and his gracious demeanor attract one towards him in an indescribable fashion, and have led me to think of him as a being apart, consecrated for the work he had in hand.

And what could be more genuinely self-revealing, as regards the absence of selfish ambition and as indicating the devoted patriotism by which the man is consumed, than these paragraphs from his own pen:

" So far it has all happened as I foretold, only the crisis has come a little more hurriedly. I expected Yuan-Shih-Kai would have been able to hold out longer. I was so full of this belief that when a year ago Yuan sent for me I distrusted his messenger. I thought he was playing false, but he was really in earnest. He wished to remove the ban from my life and act openly in concert with me. But I said to his messenger:

" ' Go back to your master and tell him I have not labored fifteen years and suffered so many perils to be tricked so easily. Tell his Excellency I can wait.'

" If I had trusted Yuan's messenger the revolution would have happened sooner, and I should now be in Peking. For I can count upon millions of followers. They will follow me to the death, as they have long followed my teachings.

* * * * *

"Whether I am to be the titular head of all China, or to work in conjunction with another, and that other Yuan-Shih-Kai, is of no importance to me. I have done my work; the wave of enlightenment and progress cannot now be stayed, and China—the country in the world most fitted to be a republic, because of the industrious and docile character of the people—will, in a short time, take her place amongst the civilized and liberty-loving nations of the world."

As a further instance of Sun's all-pervading courtesy and kindliness, I would mention an occurrence, insignificant in itself no doubt, but under the circumstances interesting. He came to my house in November, 1911, and the maid who opened the door, and who had known him for many years, gave him a smiling welcome. The chosen head of 400,000,000 of people, carrying in his pocket a telegram just received asking him to be President of the Chinese Republic, shook hands with her and cordially returned the greeting.

The story of this telegram is also of interest. It was sent from Canton and addressed to Sun Wen, London. Sun Wen is

Sun's official name, Sun Yat Sen his family name. Most Chinese have three or even four names. One the name his parents give him at birth; another the name his schoolmaster bestows upon him when he enters school; a third the young man selects for himself when he reaches adult years; and yet again he bears the name under which he is entered in the official records. The Chinese puts his family name, what we term the surname, first; and it is only the latter part of the name, which stands for our first or Christian name, which varies.

" Sun Wen, London," was rather a vague address, but the Post Office officials wrote across the envelope, " Try Chinese Legation." Thither the telegram was evidently sent, but when it was read it was forwarded on to my house with a message asking whether the person to whom it was addressed was residing there. I was not at home, but my wife, luckily, was. Many telegrams had been coming for some weeks before Sun arrived in London, and we had instructions to open them. This telegram was, of course, already open; the communication was in cipher, and after each ciphered word a Chinese character was evidently recently written. Sun had not reached our house when the telegram arrived, although we were almost hourly expecting him, so Mrs. Cantlie was able to reply that Sun Wen was not with us. Her difficulty was what to do in the matter; this might be a most important message, and one which Sun ought to be acquainted with. Yet to acknowledge Sun's advent might lead to trouble, for the Ambassador was still representing the Manchus, and he might have had instructions to secure Sun at all hazards for all we knew to the contrary. How was the difficulty to be got over? Mrs. Cantlie copied the cipher from the telegram, Chinese characters and all, and returned it by the messenger.

When Sun came in some two hours afterwards, with the scores of letters and telegrams awaiting him, Mrs. Cantlie handed him the cipher telegram referred to; he read it, smiled, and put it in his pocket. Naturally we were anxious to know what was in this telegram; but we never, in all our intimacy with Sun, asked him anything that we considered might be private, and we always begged him not to tell us anything in the nature of a secret concerning the work in which he was engaged. It was not until next day that Mrs. Cantlie referred to the telegram and told him its history; he asked who copied the Chinese characters, and was astounded, almost to unbelieving, that Mrs.

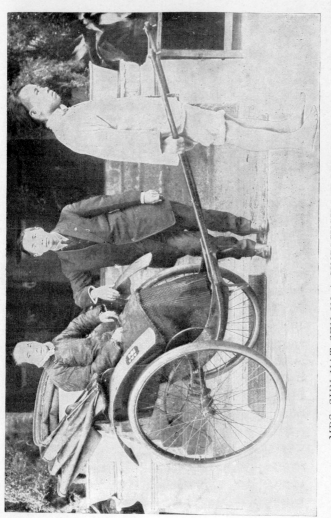

MRS. SUN YAT SEN IN A JINRICKSHA, WITH HER SON

Cantlie could have written the characters so exactly with a pen. When asked if the news was secret, " Oh no," he said, " didn't I tell you? It was asking me to be President of the new Republic."

Would any other man have received the news in the manner Sun did? I believe not. When we asked him if he would accept the presidency, he answered, after a little reflection, " Yes, for the time being, if no one else can be found better in the meantime." Probe his thoughts as we might, there never was any semblance of self-seeking. The fact that the destinies of China were in his keeping never seemed to quicken the pulse of his thoughts or disturb his equanimity. The benefit of his country was his only consideration; nothing else mattered. Neither honors, place, position, nor reward were dreamt of, far less considered. The presidency might come and go, he cared not; his country's regeneration was before all. Not that the principle he held sacred ever found expression in words; the commonplace florid oratory of the demagogue acclaiming the people's rights had no place in the category of Sun's speech or methods. Confident of success, belief in the capabilities of the men he had selected to fill the important offices of state, complete reliance upon the character of the Chinese

people to work out their own salvation, and
implicit trust in Yuan-Shih-Kai were the key-
notes of Sun's endeavor.

*   *   *   *   *

The consistent simplicity and amiability
of Sun Yat Sen's character will be gathered
from the following three letters recently received from him, and reproduced in facsimile.

Nanking,   January 21st/1912.

My Dear Dr. and Mrs. Cantlie,

It will be your pleasure to hear from me that I have assumed the Presidency of the Provisional Republican Government in China, which I accepted with disinterested fervour in order to render myself an instrumentality to rescue China with its four hundred million population from environment of impending perils and dishonour. I ought to have written you much earlier, but something or other always prevented me from doing so ; having been kept exceedingly busy since I arrived here and especially so since I occupied my present post, as you may well imagine and fairly forgive. It makes me feel more grateful to you when from the present position I look back on my past of hardships and strenuous toil, and think of your kindnesses shown me all the while that I can never nor will forget. I can say so far that the state of things here in Nanking is improving rapidly with a well founded prospect of future promise. I may not write you as often as I wish, but you may learn from the news-papers what I am doing from time to time. Kindly convey my best compliments to all my friends in London whom you know and happen to meet, and oblige.

With best wishes and kindest regards, I remain

Yours very sincerely,

Sun Yat Sen

府 統 總 國 民 華 中
REPUBLIC OF CHINA
THE PRESIDENT'S OFFICE,

Nanking, March 3rd/1912.

My dear Doctor Cantlie,

I have your very kind and interesting letter which gives me a great deal of pleasure.

I am well. Now that I have resigned in favour of Yuan Shi-kai, since my work of revolution is completed, I hope to be relieved of office soon. But, I fear, things may yet take a less favourable turn and require my service a little longer. No doubt you have seen in the last two days' papers about the riot in Peking, this calls for the greatest attention and needs immediate action to prevent it to spread further. I hope however everything will resume its normal course before long.

Yours sincerely,

Sun Yat Sen.

府 統 總 國 民 華 中
REPUBLIC OF CHINA
THE PRESIDENT'S OFFICE.

Nanking, March 12th/1912.

Dear Mrs. Cantlie,

Your welcome letter of February 18th afforded me great pleasure, and it is indeed a delight to see the familiar hand-writing again.

It is true that the Tai Ching dynasty is "a thing of the past" but the dethronement of the Manchus does not mean the complete salvation of China. We have an enormous amount of work ahead of us, and it must be accomplished in order that she may be ranked as a great power, among the family of nations.

I thank you for your earnest prayers offered in my behalf. I am glad to tell you that we are going to have religious toleration in China, and I'm sure that Christianity will flourish under the new regime.

I am going to Canton shortly and there try to convert the old city into a new and modern one.

My family is in Nanking with me. My son will return to America for his education, and I am contemplating sending my elder daughter along with her brother for the same purpose. If they should come to England I shall ask them to make it a point to call on you and the doctor.

I close this letter with my kindest regards and best wishes to you and Dr. Cantlie, I remain,

Yours sincerely,

Sun Yat Sen

III

THE RISE OF A GREAT TYRANNY

TO understand aright the Chinese Revolution—the most remarkable event surely of our time—we must realize the nature of the forces opposing Sun Yat Sen and his supporters. We must find out, in fact, upon what the Manchus based their apparently impregnable despotism. The story is a fascinating one—almost as fascinating as it is sinister. In nothing is it more remarkable than this: that while the Manchus, once upon the Chinese throne, professed to be opposed inexorably to change, and determined to preserve intact and at all costs the institutions of the country, and while to all appearance they succeeded in doing so, yet in actual fact they contrived, all unsuspected, to transmute the whole character of China's government and civilization. In this single fact we have the key to a dominion as mysterious as it was powerful —the dominion of a barbaric Tartar clan over an ancient empire. That their Manchu rulers were foreigners was always keenly felt by the Chinese. Most wisely, therefore, did the Manchus show all the deference proper in foreigners to Chinese forms of government, but none the less did they change the spirit of that government as completely as if they had thrown everything into the melting-pot. It is no exaggeration to say that the Empire Sun Yat Sen has overthrown was more alien to that of his forefathers than the Republic he has established, and the great achievement of the Revolution has been to restore China to her true, her normal self.

It is easy to explain this paradox. Consider for a moment the working of the normal Chinese autocracy in the pre-Manchu days. It was absolutely different to all the despotisms of the East. Such a thing, for instance, as the sudden elevation by the Emperor of grooms and barbers to high official posts was as unknown to China as it was familiar, say, to Turkey or Persia. The Chinese had found out the competitive examination, and in the old days it was only by hard and successful study that a Chinese could climb from the lowest step of the official ladder to the higher rounds. The principle that good government consisted in getting the services of the best men, of the " heen nang "—the " worthy

and talented," " the good and able "—was
firmly rooted in the Chinese mind; which
reasoned that, although there could be no
degrees, no bachelorships, no doctorates of
virtue, yet, as there was an intimate con-
nection between moral and intellectual elevation, so the competitive examination afforded
the best available test of the fittest men to
govern. The test may have been imperfect,
crude even, but at least it was honestly ad-
ministered, and behind it lay the idea that
government to be effective must be entrusted
to the fittest, that no pains must be spared
to discover and reward these, and that, once
found, the power and responsibility must be
theirs. The Chinese were free from the de-
lusion that the qualities which make a capable
administrator or a wise governor are hereditary. Never did they hold that the control
of the Empire should be vested largely in
the members of one class. Fitness, not birth,
was the essential, and, as the only method
of discovering fitness was by the competitive
examinations, immense importance attached
to these functions. Thousands of candidates
attended them, representing every class of
the community. The very office of Emperor,
it should be noted, was by no means hereditary. The pure theory of succession was that
the best and wisest man in the Empire should

be nominated. This became so far modified in practice that the Emperor selected his ablest son, taking no account of priority of birth, whilst if the said son failed to show conspicuous qualities for governorship, his deposition was not very difficult to arrange. The military and police maintained were sufficient to crush merely factious risings, but quite inadequate to put down a general rising on the part of an indignant people. In a word, Chinese government was probably the most scientific attempt ever made to secure government by aristocracy—using the word in its pure sense, $\alpha\rho\iota\sigma\tau\sigma$, the best.

Then came the Manchus. The last representative of the Ming dynasty had not been a success. Probably he was in his own person a disproof of the adequacy of the aristocratic theory of government, for he has been denounced as being given over to sensual indulgence and as inattentive to the affairs of state. In any case he was not popular. Rebellion raged, and the victorious rebel leader, Le Tsze Ching, at last entered Peking at the head of his conquering army— to find that the Ming Emperor, deserted and unsupported, had committed suicide. And then occurred one of the tragedies of history. One of the Ming Generals, a certain Woo San Kwei, was then on the borders of

China endeavoring with indifferent success
to keep off an invasion of the Manchu Tartar
clans. It was harder apparently to Woo
San to submit to his rebel countryman than
to the foreign invader. In any case, he
sought the Manchu's aid to oust the usurper.
It was given. Seven years' war followed—
seven years compared to which, one authority
says, the Seven Years' Prussian War was
a trifle! At the end the rebels were crushed
—and the reign of the Manchus began, and
with it the decadence of the Chinese Empire.

We have said that the Manchus were
scrupulous to observe the forms of the
Chinese Government. More, they made no
attempt to impugn its theory. The admin-
istration of the country by the best and best-
trained men was still, they agreed, desirable.
The competitive examinations to discover
who these were continued to be held '' under
distinguished auspices.'' There was one
trifling difference, however. The Manchus
found themselves under the necessity of
maintaining a huge standing army. Revolt
was still smoldering, and had to be put down
with an iron hand. A huge Tartar garrison
was massed at Peking. Smaller garrisons
were appointed at nine of the provincial capitals and ten other important points. The
very sight of these garrisons has been for

over two hundred years a reminder to the
Chinese that they were under the heel of a
foreign dominion, and has served to exacer-
bate them over and over again. That by
the way, however. The point is that the
garrisons proved, with their numerous prog-
eny, very costly to maintain, and then there
grew up the system which has since developed
to a fine art—the sale of public offices. The
students still competed and held their examinations, but, if afterwards they desired any
considerable appointment, they had to pay
for it. Thus did the Manchus raise their
revenue! Corruption spread throughout the
whole of the Civil Service of China till there
was no one to corrupt. And with corruption
came another change. The ancient government of China was marked by a high degree
of centralization. There was a constant re-
vision by the Emperor and his ministers of
the acts of all the military, fiscal and judicial
services. Governors and mandarins were re-
movable at his pleasure, and each and all of
them knew that, at any moment, they might
be called upon to give an account of their
stewardship. But with the Manchu ascend-
ancy this system of centralized control gave
way to a corrupt feudalism. There ceased
to be any real check upon the mandarins.
Huge provinces were at the mercy of some

grasping governor, who had only bought his appointment to " squeeze " the people, and was, therefore, entitled to " squeeze " them as hard as he could. For the only official remuneration worth thinking of was, as we have seen, that which the officials themselves blackmailed from the public. Under the Manchus, in fact, the Court sold the right to " squeeze " to all scholars who would pay for it, and the old Chinese Government, which, with all its crudities and imperfections, was yet animated by the guiding impulse of a great idea, was utterly destroyed for ever. With the increase of the Manchu race, the necessity of providing for them became apparent. Accordingly they had the refusal of the most lucrative appointments and were put in control of the most important provinces, with the most populous cities and fertile lands. From their decisions there was no effective appeal. In a thousand ways they bled the people and practised extortion at every possible opportunity. As the corruption intensified, so did the standard of competence fall, until at last, as the whole land passed under the Manchus, the Chinese, taught by centuries of custom and religion to revere the law and its officers, found that, while their idol remained outwardly the same, fair seeming and good to look upon, its heart had changed to that of a devil. They struggled hard against the Manchus, and in spirit never accepted them. South-East China, where the present revolution took its rise, was ever bitterly anti-Manchu. " For about forty years," says Mr. Taylor Meadows, " after the advent of the Manchu dynasty was proclaimed at Peking, the mountaineers and coastlanders of South-Eastern China never felt themselves completely and hopelessly under its sway; and from that date to the present day—during a period of 170 years—this very portion of China has been the great seat of a formidable political society, best known as the ' San Ho Hwuy '— the Triad Society—the express object of which has been the expulsion of the barbarian conquerors of their country."

All that time " Fan Tsing fuh Ming " remained their motto (" Overthrow the Manchus, re-establish the Mings "). But the Manchus were too strong. They had seized the throne at a moment when China was divided and weakened by long and bitter civil war. They kept it by an outward compliance with Chinese custom, adroitly altered to suit their own policy, and they backed their position with such a military force as the poor Chinese were unable to dispute.

One signal advantage the early Manchus

possessed. Their first Emperors were men
of real ability—able if unscrupulous, realiz-
ing to the full that much depended upon their
own sagacity and conduct. But as time
brought a deeper sense of security, a new
type of ruler appeared—arrogant and idle,
given over to the trivialities of life, openly
contemptuous of the people who acknowl-
edged his sway. This is not surprising.
The Chinese Emperor, it must be remembered, is, or rather he was, the " Son of
Heaven," the " Supreme Ruler," the " August Lofty One," the " Celestial Ruler," the
" Solitary Man," the " Buddha of the Present Day "; and, in adulatory addresses, he
was often hailed the " Lord of Ten Thousand
Years."

" In harmony with these lofty attributes,
his subjects," says Sir R. K. Douglas in " Society in China," " when admitted into his
presence, prostrate themselves in adoration
on the ground before him, and on a certain
day in the year he is worshipped in every
city in the Empire. At daylight, on the day
in question, the local mandarins assemble in
the city temple, where, in the central hall, a
throne is raised on which is placed the imperial tablet. At a given signal the assembled officials kneel thrice before the throne,
and nine times strike their heads on the

ground as though in the presence of the Supreme Ruler.''

'' With the exception of those immediately
about his person, his subjects are not allowed
to gaze upon his face. When he goes abroad
the people are compelled to fall on their faces
to the ground until his cavalcade has passed
on, and on all occasions he is to them a mystery.''

'' The palace, as befitting the abode of so
exalted a personage, is so placed as effectu-
ally to cut off its occupants from the rest of
the Empire. Situated in the ' Forbidden
City,' it is surrounded with a triple barrier
of walls. Beyond the inner and arcane en-
closure is the imperial city, which is en-
closed by a high wall topped with tiles of the
imperial yellow color; and outside that again
is the Tartar city, which forms the northern
part of the capital. Strict guard is kept
night and day at the gates of the Forbidden
City, and severe penalties are inflicted on all
unauthorized persons who may dare to enter
its portals.'' Only on rare occasions, and
those almost exclusively occasions of ceremony, does the Emperor pass out of the
palace grounds. '' These no doubt present a
microcosm of the Empire. There are lakes,
mountains, parks, and gardens in which the
imperial prisoner can amuse himself, with

the boats which ply on the artificial water,
or by joining mimic hunts in miniature forests; but it is probable that there is not one
of the millions of China who has not more
practical knowledge of the Empire than he
who rules it. Theoretically he is supposed
to spend his days and nights in the affairs of
state."[1] As Sir Robert Douglas observes:
" It is only men of the strongest will and
keenest intellects who would not rust under
such conditions, and these qualities are possessed as rarely by Emperors as by ordinary
persons."

And with the Manchus, once the stimulus
of their accession had worn off, those qualities became rare indeed. Vigilance gave
way to sensual sloth. Stories of vicious de-
pravity upon the part of Emperor after Emperor became common gossip through China.
More and more, the central authority slack-
ened and the mandarins waxed fat as their
extortions increased. If rebellion was attempted it was crushed with pitiless force.
The people were forbidden knowledge.
Whereas under the old dispensation complete
copies of the law could be cheaply and easily
procured, a time came when the laws were
to be known only to the highest officials and
forbidden to public eyes. In fact, as

[1] "Society in China," by Sir R. K. Douglas.

the central power relaxed, as decadent Emperor succeeded decadent, so the grip of the mandarins upon the people tightened, until the vast and complicated machinery of the Chinese Government became one great engine of oppression, whose officers had but one idea—the "squeezing" of the common people.

There is a certain story, gruesome yet fascinating, by Edgar Allan Poe, which illustrates vividly the conditions into which the Manchu despotism gradually fell. A man sick unto death is hypnotized, and while hypnotized and sitting erect in his chair, dies. Hours pass and the watchers see no change, till they go to rouse him, and find that he is dead—dead in the same attitude as when the hypnotist commanded him to sit up. It was much like this with the Manchu Empire. Looking back upon the history of that dynasty now, it is easy to see that decay had set in long ago, and that, though to all outward appearance strong and erect, its springs of action had long since dried up, so that the end in fact was not far off. But there was this difference between the Manchus and Poe's hypnotized man. When the shock of outside reality came to the Manchus, they at least had sufficient vitality to pull themselves together for one last desperate effort—an effort that came within an ace of succeeding.

And the shock was the aggression of Europe. As the nations became more and more convinced of the magnitude of the Chinese market, they sent envoys to the Celestial Empire in the hope of creating a good understanding. The good understanding did not follow. There ensued instead interminable delays, refusals to negotiate, and insane restrictions; until at last came the war with Great Britain, and British artillery crashed into the consciousness of the sleeping Chinese, who was galvanized into a sudden activity. The blow to the Manchus was staggering. Their provincial garrisons were defeated and almost destroyed with an ease that shook their confidence in the prowess and destiny of their great race, and smashed its prestige to pieces. They were disgraced before their conquered subjects; but the blow saved them, at any rate for a time. The Court of Peking was roused as it had not been for two hundred years. A season of feverish activity followed; inquiries were instituted as to the condition of the country. The Emperor gave frequent audiences to the mandarins. There is on record the report of an examination by the Emperor Tao-Kuang, so full of interest and throwing so valuable

a light upon the Chinese point of view, that
we set it out in full:—

AUDIENCE ON THE 11TH DAY.

Emperor. Do you think from the appearance of things at Kwang-tung that the British barbarians or any other people will cause
trouble again?

Answer. No. Britain itself has got nothing, and when the British barbarians rebelled
in 1841, they depended entirely on the power
of the other nations, who, with a view to
open trade, supported them with funds. In
the present year the (here follow two words
which do not make sense with the context,
" teen te," literally " laws and territory ";
probably " subject territories " were the
words used) of Britain yield her no willing
obedience.

Emperor. It is plain from this that these
barbarians always look on trade as their chief
occupation, and are wanting in any high purpose of striving for territorial acquisitions.

Answer. At bottom they belong to the
class of brutes (dogs and horses); it is impossible they should have any high purpose.

Emperor. Hence in their country they
have now a woman, now a man as their prince
(wang). It is plain they are not worth at-

tending to. Have they got like us any fixed time of service for their soldier's head?

Answer. Some are changed once in two years, some once in three years. Although it is the prince of these barbarians who sends them, they are in reality recommended by the body of their merchants.

Emperor. What goods do the French trade in?

Answer. The wares of the barbarians are only camlets, woollen cloth, clocks, watches, cottons, and the like. All the countries have got them good or bad.

Emperor. What country's goods are dearest?

Answer. They have all got both dear and cheap. There is no great difference in their prices (of similar articles); only with respect to the camlets, the French are said to be the best.

Emperor. China has no want of silk fabrics and cottons; what necessity is there for using foreign cottons in particular? For instance, wrappers can be made of yellow or pale yellow (for the palace), and people outside could see Nanking clock colored, or blue ones. This would look simple and unaffected; but lately foreign flowered cottons have come into use which look very odd. Others use foreign cottons for shirts. Now

MARKET PLACE IN FULL BLAST
IN MARKET-TOWN OF LAI-PU-SUA NEAR KITYANG

observe me—the highest of men—my shirts and inner garments are all made of Corean cottons. I have never used foreign cottons.

Answer. Foreign cotton cloth has no substance (literally bone), it is not good for clothing.

Emperor. And it does not wash well.

Answer. Yes, Sire.

Emperor. I suppose opium is bought and sold quite openly in Kwang-tung.

Answer. I should not dare to deceive your Majesty—people do not dare to buy and sell it openly, but there is no small quantity bought and sold secretly.

Emperor. It appears to me that in this matter too there must be a flourishing period and a period of decay. Even if I were to inflict severe punishments, I might punish to-day and punish again to-morrow, and all without benefit. If we wait for two or three years—for five or six years—it will of course fall into disuse of itself.

Answer. Certainly, Sire.

Emperor. How is it with the levying and payment of the taxes in Kwang-tung? How do matters stand as to deficiencies in the district treasuries?

Answer. In Kwang-tung the fixed regular land tax is paid up annually; as to the miscellaneous taxes—I do not dare to deceive your Majesty—there must have been some appropriated for public purposes.

Emperor. Can these appropriations not be avoided then? You will do very well for a superintendent of finances. To-morrow present your name for an audience.

AUDIENCE ON THE 12TH DAY.

Emperor. In your opinion is opium dearer or cheaper now than in former years? (Smiling.) You don't smoke it—I fear you cannot tell.

Answer. The local gentry and *literati* of whom I have inquired state that opium is very cheap at present.

Emperor. Indeed. Why is it cheap?

Answer. Because its quality is not equal to what it was formerly.

Emperor. This, now, is an example of prosperity and decay! How could heaven and earth long endure an article so destructive to human life? So, in the consumption of tobacco the Kwang-tung leaf being strong tasted, the Singtsze weak, those who have accustomed themselves to the strong do not of course like the weak. Do you think that in future the British barbarians in Hong Kong will go on quietly or not?

Answer. The British barbarians have

gone to great expenses in building houses
with the view of permanently residing there,
and living in quiet. Besides, the people of
Hong Kong and its neighborhood took at an
early period an aversion to these barbarians;
and local bandits have long been waiting,
their mouths watering for the place. The
barbarians are therefore constantly in dread,
fearing they may lose it.

Emperor. So they have added to their
troubles by giving to themselves another internal care. However, notwithstanding this,
they have always got their own country for
a haunt (literally, nest and den, expressions
frequently applied to the capitals of foreign
sovereigns).

Answer. Yes, Sire.

Emperor. Have the Governor-General
and the Governor any difference of opinion
or not?

Answer. Your slave intreats your Majesty to set your sacred mind at rest—the
Governor-General and the Governor not only
transact their business in strict good faith,
but in all cases without disagreement.

Emperor. That is well. What is wanted
is agreement; frequently the Governor-General and the Governor in the same province
are at variance.

Answer. Your slave, during the many

years he has been in Kwang-tung, has never witnessed so much concord between the Governor-General and the Governor.

Emperor. They are both in their best years, just the time for exertion; they ought to do their utmost physically and mentally. It is right, too, that you and the criminal judge, their immediate subordinates, when you learn anything of which you fear they may not be thoroughly informed, should tell them all you know. Are you acquainted with the newly appointed judge, Ke shuh tsaou?

Answer. No, Sire.

Emperor. He is a very honest, sincere, and unaffected man, as you will know after you have passed half a year in the same place with him. You can make ready for your departure. How long will you be on the journey?

Answer. Upwards of two months.

Emperor. I reckon that you will arrive about the end of the 11th or the beginning of the 12th month. Or, allowing a few days more, you will reach Canton about the middle of the 12th month.

Thus far had the Manchu intelligence evolved in the middle of the last century. Ludicrous as the Emperor's comments appear, they yet mark a distinct advance on

his previous attitude, for the curiosity and
apprehension he evinced was more hopeful
than the blank and utter indifference it succeeded. But, as will be easily understood,
the statecraft of such a ruler was not equal
to the needs of the situation—a situation that
increased in difficulty and complexity. For
there followed the most formidable rising the
Manchus had been called upon to face—the
famous Taiping Rebellion, and then, close
upon its heels, the war of 1861, with the
ceding to Britain of the adjacent peninsula
of Kowloon—events that call for more than
passing notice, for they both contributed in
a marked degree to the revolution that has
recently startled the world.

IV

THE LAST OF THE MANCHUS

THE Taiping Rebellion broke out in 1850. Not till 1864 was it subdued. During twelve of the intervening sixteen years, Nanking, the capital of Southern China, was in the hands of the rebels. Over a dozen provinces were devastated, hundreds of cities were captured. In a score of pitched battles the imperial troops suffered defeat. Quite obviously Manchu generalship was wholly unequal to the task before it. " The rebels," wrote an officer, " increase more and more; they are powerful and fierce, their regulations and laws being rigorous and clear. Our troops, the more they fight, the more they fear! They have not a tincture of discipline. Retreating is easy to them, advancing difficult." Small wonder that the cry, " Exterminate the Manchus! "—a cry, by the way, raised during this very revolution, and silenced only by the authority of Sun Yat Sen—began to penetrate into the palace of Peking, and broke upon the startled

ear of the Emperor with a new significance.

Aid was yet to come to the Manchus, however, and from a strange quarter. While the
rebellion still raged and threatened, war
broke out, and once again Britain and France
determined to punish China—this time perhaps not in so righteous a cause. The armies
that could not hold their own against the
Taipings offered but a feeble resistance to
the Allies, who swept all before them,
marched on Peking, from whence the Court
had fled, burnt to the ground the famous
Summer Palace, and, in a word, humbled
China to the dust.

It is not surprising that at this juncture,
with the rebellion rife, with the capital in
the hands of the foreigner, and the Emperor
himself a weak debauchee, upon the point
of death, the view gained ground among the
literati and writers that the dynasty was
doomed, or, as they put it, with admirable
politeness, "It had exhausted the mandate
of heaven." The fortunes of the Manchus
looked desperate indeed. Their armies
broken, their prestige shattered, exiled from
their own Court, their very lives were in constant danger. It was at this crisis that a
new personality made itself felt amongst
them—a personality destined to exercise a

decisive influence on the fortunes of the country.

Upon the death of the Emperor Tao-Kuang in 1850—he whose engaging conversations we have recorded in the last chapter—his eldest surviving son, aged nineteen, ascended the throne under the reign-title of Hsien-Feng. The period of mourning over, a decree was issued constituting the Emperor's harem. All beautiful Manchu maidens were to present themselves at the Imperial Household office with a view to a first selection being made. The Chinese, it will be noted, were exempt from contributing to the choice, owing to the fact that the royal race persistently intermarried—an offence they held in abhorrence. Among those who came in tripping obedience to the nuptial command was the young Yehonala, the daughter of a cadet branch of the royal family. The inner economy of the Manchu household decrees that the mother of the Emperor should select her son's consorts, and Yehonala found favor with the old lady. She was appointed a concubine of the rank of Kuei Jen, or "honorable person"; and, launched on her career at Court, she did her utmost to gain the goodwill of every one who could serve an ambition that was already inordinate.

She had not long to wait. The Emperor
was childless and known to be in broken
health, and when, therefore, she presented
him with a son, the event was one of national
importance. The authority she obtained as
mother of the heir apparent was instantly
felt. Her colleague, the Empress Consort
(who was of course the Emperor's official
wife), took little or no active interest in the
business of government. The Emperor,
stricken with paralysis, soon broke down
completely, and Yehonala became the real
ruler of the Chinese Empire. All the business of the imperial city and of the Empire
came to depend upon her word, and in a
country where no woman is supposed
to rule, a young girl of twenty-two was
paramount.

It is strangely interesting to watch the first
manifestations of the fierce spirit that for
sixty years was to control the destinies of
China. At once she arrested the downward
course of things. She stopped, always of
course in the Emperor's name, the negotia-
tions for peace with Britain and France, and
issued the most vigorous edict which had proceeded from the Manchu throne for years.
It explained that:—" Any further forbearance on our part would be a dereliction of
our duty to the Empire, so that we have now

commanded our armies to attack them—*i.e.,*
the barbarians—with all possible energy, and
we have now directed the local gentry to organize trained bands, and with them either
to join in the attack or to block the barbarians' advance. Hereby we make offer of
the following rewards: For the head of a
black barbarian 50 taels, and for the head of
a white barbarian 100 taels; for the capture
of a barbarian leader, alive or dead, 500
taels; and for the seizure or destruction of a
barbarian vessel 5,000 taels. The inhabitants
of Tientsin are reputed brave. Let them
now come forward and rid us of these pesti-
lential savages, either by open attack or by
artifice. We are no lovers of war, but all
our people must admit that this has been
forced on us.''

'' The barbarians' superiority,'' another
edict explained, '' lies in their firearms, but
if we could only bring them to a hand-to-hand
engagement they will be unable to get their
artillery to bear, and thus shall our victory
be assured. The Mongolian Manchu horsemen are quite useless for this kind of warfare, but the men of Hupei and Ssŭ-ch'uan
are as agile as monkeys and adepts at the
use of cover in secret approaches. Let them
but surprise these bandits once, and their
rout is inevitable . . . for bravery and

good service there will be great rewards. A most important decree."

Shortsighted and futile as these decrees appear, there breathed in them a new spirit of resolution and of purpose that had an immediate effect upon the Chinese temperament, and raised their real author high in official estimation. True, they were followed by an inglorious surrender and an almost abject peace—an inevitable result that statesmen would have foreseen. But it is not always statecraft and a wide vision of affairs that impresses Eastern, or for the matter of that Western, peoples, so much as tenacity and pluck. Yehonala soon gave plenty of evidence of both these qualities. At Jehol, where the Emperor lay dying, affairs had fallen somewhat under the dominion of Prince Yi, with whom were associated as Grand Councillors the Prince Tuan Hua and the imperial clansman Su Shun. These three noblemen, recognizing that the Emperor's end was near and that a Regency would be necessary, determined on securing that power for themselves. Prince Yi was nominally the leader of this conspiracy, but its instigator was Su Shun. Su Shun had an immense fortune. It had been at his instance that the Secretaries of the Board of Revenue had been cashiered on a charge of making illicit profits.

Upon this accusation he had obtained the
arrest of over one hundred notables and rich
merchants, and kept them in custody of no
gentle kind until they had been ransomed
with enormous sums. It was thus that there
was founded a fortune so enormous that, as
we shall see, it survived even the extrava-
gance of the Chinese Court for over half a
century.

There can be no doubt that Su Shun's
possession of this vast fortune was no incon-
siderable factor in shaping the conduct of
Yehonala. Apparently she made no effort
to combat the influence of the three conspirators on the dying Emperor, but she
thoughtfully abstracted the seal which, kept
in the personal custody of the Emperor and
bearing the characters " lawfully trans-
mitted authority," is absolutely necessary
to establish the authenticity of the first edict
of a new reign, confident that, when the death
of the Emperor came, the advantage would
remain with her. When the Emperor passed
away, Su Shun and his friends found themselves saddled with another dilemma. Either
as Regents they had to escort the royal bier
back to Peking or to outrage etiquette and
opinion by leaving it to take care of itself
and hurrying back to the capital. They
shrank from this course, which would have

ranged against them both Chinese and Manchu feeling. This gave Yehonala her chance.
The funeral cortège necessarily made slow
progress. Hers was rapid. She reached the
capital some days before the Regents, and
at once busied herself with the task of giving
them a warm reception, enlisting very readily
the help of Pince Kung, the Emperor's uncle,
whom, as she ascertained, the conspirators
intended to execute. When Su Shun and his
friends arrived at Peking they found Yehonala in possession. The troops, the nobles,
the officials, all were on her side. They were
seized and imprisoned. Pince Yi and Prince
Yuan were " permitted to commit suicide,"
and Su Shun was decapitated. Thus did Yehonala inaugurate her reign—nominally,
that of her son—of " All-Pervading Tran-
quillity! "

At first the words seemed not ill-chosen.
Peace was concluded with the Allies. The
Taipings were defeated and finally crushed
by Gordon, who lent his services to the
Chinese Government. A wise ruler would
have seized the opportunity to inaugurate
some of those reforms that, it was even then
glaringly apparent, China stood in urgent
need of. But the Empress Dowager recked
little of reform. She was a typical Manchu, bold, alert, resourceful, but knowing lit-

tle and caring less for foreign ideas or Western notions. She was on the throne of China, mistress of the vastest empire in the world. To cement her power she had the vast fortune of Su Shun, some of whose millions, it is said, still lie in the vaults at the palace.[1] Little by little her authority grew, until it transcended the power of any of the Manchu Emperors of the past. It became a dangerous matter to oppose her will. Those who did so were one by one removed. Prince Kung was the first to feel her displeasure. The incident is thus related by Messrs. Bland and Backhouse in their " China under the Empress Dowager." " In a moment of absentmindedness or bravado Prince Kung ventured to rise from his knee during an audience, thus violating a fundamental rule of etiquette originally instituted to guard the Sovereign against any sudden attack. The attendant eunuchs promptly informed their Majesties " (who, it should be noted, spoke to their ministers from behind a curtain), " whereupon the Empress Dowager called loudly for help, exclaiming that the Prince was about to execute some evil treachery against the person of the Regents. The

[1] They were, at all events, found there on the return of the Court to Peking in 1900, after the flight following the Boxer rebellion.

guards rushed in and Prince Kung was ordered to leave the royal presence.'' Later he was suspended from his high office, '' because,'' said the edict, '' his rebellious and usurping tendencies must be sternly checked.'' Others were less fortunate than Prince Kung. The Empress Tzŭ An, her co-Regent, yielding and conciliatory to a degree, yet lived to incur the Empress Dowager's displeasure. She fell ill of a sudden and mysterious sickness. Her death was generally attributed to poison, and no one had any doubts as to the poisoner.

Blacker deeds than poison have been established against the Empress Dowager. Her son, when he attained his majority, thus ending the Regency, refused to submit state documents for her inspection. There were serious differences—and an early death of the Emperor. '' All commentators,'' say Messrs. Bland and Backhouse, '' agree that the Empress Dowager encouraged the youthful Emperor's tendencies to dissipated habits, but when these had resulted in a serious illness she allowed it to work havoc with his delicate constitution without providing him with such medical assistance as might have been available.'' Worse remains. The young Emperor left a wife, A-lu-te, who at the time of his death was *enceinte*. Now, in

the event of the Emperor's child succeeding
his dead father, the Empress Dowager's
power would have been gone, because the
Empress A-lu-te would have then become
Empress Dowager and would have secured
the Regency. Accordingly, the Dowager
Empress insisted on the election of another
infant Emperor at all costs and in violation
of the law of dynastic succession. The infant
son of Prince Ch'un was selected for the
throne. A-lu-te, her own child born, committed suicide, and the " Old Buddha," as
Yehonala had come to be called by the people, was left in supreme authority.

But, jealous as she was of power, there
were those who obtained enormous influence
over her and through her on the Empire.
One of the grossest evils of Chinese government—an evil that under the Empress Dowager obtained dreadful dimensions—is the
demoralizing influence of the eunuch system
on the Court and its immediate entourage.
There has scarcely been a reformer in China
who has not placed first the abolition of this
system, now swept away at last with the
dynasty on which it battened. It is difficult,
nay impossible, to say how much mischief
has been caused in the past by these irre-
sponsible advisers of the Throne. It is said

that the Boxer risings, and the support given
them by the Empress Dowager, were both
dictated by the part which her favorite eunuch, Li-Lien-Ying, played in fomenting
opinion against the foreigners. Who can
tell? But the power of the eunuchs, ubiquitous and insistent, with their constant access
to the person of the Sovereign, their intimate
knowledge of that Sovereign's tastes and
moods, was no doubt immense, and throughout the Empress Dowager's reign, while she
remained utterly irresponsive to representa-
tions from outside the Forbidden City, while,
for instance, she could not be moved by the
earnest appeal of men so capable as Li-
Hung-Chang or Yuan-Shi-Kai, yet to the
whispers of the palace eunuchs she lent a
ready ear.

The inner history of the Celestial Empire
and of the Manchu dynasty is inextricably
bound up with the eunuchs and their far-
reaching intrigues. During the half-century
of the Empress Dowager's rule, the power
behind the throne, literally a power of darkness in high places, was that of her favorite
chamberlains. There were not wanting obvious explanations of their influence. It was
said that the chief eunuch, Te Hai, only nominally answered to that description, and
that, in fact, the Empress Dowager had had

a son by him—a son whose birth pamphleteers record with much detail—who is said to be still abroad in the land. More, strange and dreadful stories of nameless depravities committed in the palace spread through Southern China. The licentious festivities of the Court were the subject of many a rival ballad. Tales of wild orgies began to be circulated. No one can doubt that the Empress Dowager, now she felt her position established, surrendered herself to a life of unrestrained excesses, tempered only by such attention to affairs as was necessary to retain her own supremacy. Remonstrance proved vain. The cynical and selfish woman who sat upon the throne of China was an adept in misleading opinion, and to the memorials of the Censor she replied by edicts impressive only to those who did not know the facts. '' At a time like this,'' she wrote, '' when rebellions are still raging, and our people are in sore distress, when our treasuries are empty, and our revenues insufficient for the needs of government, our hearts are heavy with sorrowful thoughts, and must be so, especially as long as His late Majesty's remains have not yet been borne to their final resting-place. How, then, could we possibly permit such a state of things as the Censor describes?''

And so the solemn farce went on. In admirable language the Empress enjoined virtue, and continued to practise the most flagrant vice. And outside the Forbidden City millions of impoverished Chinese worked their fingers to the bone that they might minister to her depraved pleasures. For those pleasures the public services were drained of money; the very Navy itself was, on the advice of the chief eunuch, starved for years in order that the Empress might continue the building of her Summer Palace, and once again the arms of China had to suffer dishonor—this time by Japan—to gratify the luxurious whims of a woman, the price of whose self-indulgence was the degradation of her people.

And all the time the tigress was on the pounce, quick to scent hostility to herself and unsparing in her measures to suppress it. She had that indescribable quality which inspires blind steadfast obedience in others, and she was an excellent judge of men, cool in danger and never deceived by adulation. Add to this the fact that the great masses of China were still sunk in fathomless ignorance, without leaders, with no clue to the reason of their own impoverishment and misery, unconscious indeed of anything beyond, and it becomes less miraculous that this indomitable woman sat secure on her throne —the last of a doomed dynasty.

But keen as was her vision, its range was narrow and restricted, and the Old Buddha did not perceive that there were at work in China forces that could not be disregarded with any safety. First, there was a new movement stirring among the choked populace of Canton, a movement that was charged with all the old hostility to the Manchus, but tinged also with broad democratic ideas that went far beyond the restoration of another dynasty. It has been that movement which Dr. Sun Yat Sen, the Carnot of the revolution, has guided to victory. Essentially democratic in its character, it saw no deliverance for China unless the people were roused.

Far removed from it in sympathy, but yet of unmistakable significance, was the growing feeling among men of a different stamp that if the partition of China was to be prevented, the time for reorganization had arrived. It was apparent, woefully apparent, even to Viceroys so cautious as Li-Hung-Chang or Yuan-Shi-Kai, that the reforming hand was needed, not only so far as the Army and Navy were concerned, but even more as regards China's educational services; and as they found all their plans defeated and their influence checkmated by the intrigues of

A TYPICAL ANCESTRAL TEMPLE at Hun Lou, near Swatow

the palace eunuchs, or when they were snubbed for their pains by the Empress, still unyielding and undiscerning, they asked themselves, in despair of the ancient *régime,* if the time had not come for a Limited Monarchy and Representative Government. By degrees the number of dissatisfied officials increased. All that was vital, all that was patriotic in the Chinese bureaucracy ranged itself on the side of reform. A time had come when its urgency could no longer be denied, and the ablest and most trusted servants of the Executive besought the Throne to put its house in order.

What was the result? Merely this: that they were marked men to be got rid of at the first opportunity; and the last state of that bureaucracy, in which only the effete and the decadent could succeed, was worse than the first. The Reform Party it was who gained what officialdom lost.

But though the Empress remained deaf to all appeals, that party found an enthusiastic and powerful convert.

Kuang Hsü, the son of Prince Ch'un, had come to the throne, and at one moment of his reign it seemed as if there were at long last to be some relief for the parched millions of China, some hope again for the lost grandeur of the Middle Kingdom. For the young Emperor lent an ear to those who insisted that it was only by change, drastic and immediate, that the deplorable state of the country and her defences could be amended. Kuang Hsü has been described, for some strange reason, as a decadent, perhaps because that word is a convenient term of opprobrium to describe those whose aims we dislike. The policy he initiated, however, smacked little of decadence. Its faults were those of youth, of inexperience, of an energy that recked too little of consequences and that despised its enemies too heartily to measure their strength.

For ten long years after his accession, and although the Empress Dowager had gone through the pretence of resignation, she still held the reins in her hands. True, she did not consult either ministers or scholars. Her Court came to consist only of eunuchs, a few Manchus, and one or two ministers of the imperial household. The most serious study she engaged in was that of private theatricals, for which she had a passion. But she still pulled the wires, and her veto continually blocked the way. All the ministers of the first and second degree were her nominees; all were feeble and aged men, dreading the idea of change, which would end their positions, and bent only on putting difficulties in the way of reform. The Emperor, in fact, had no power. At every step he was checkmated. He saw his country humiliated again and again. Port Arthur, Ta-Lien-Wan and Formosa were lost in succession. The Empress Dowager was unconcerned. The Summer Palace and her pleasures were left her and for the rest she was indifferent. But as it happened, the Emperor did care. " I will never be the ruler of a perishing empire," he declared. " If I have no power, I had better abdicate." First, however, he determined he would make one effort for his people while there was yet time.

He reasoned that if he allowed things to take their course, the ruin of the Empire was inevitable. A bold policy might save the situation. Even if it failed, the attempt would be worth making and might arouse the people. There is something infinitely pathetic in the struggle of this young man, surrounded on all sides with the hostile agents of the Empress Dowager, with his ministers thwarting him at every step, his very servants spying on his conversations, able only to take counsel with his friends by stealth and at odd moments, with scarcely one honest and responsible minister ready to help him, and with the whole Court ready to betray him at the first false step. Despite all, he persisted.

He was under no illusions as to the probability of his own defeat, but he was resolved to take the risk.

"Let the farce of ruling go," he wrote; "let poison, let assassination come. With death, I shall deliver up my imperial charge. With death, I shall report myself to my ancestors. With death, I shall be worthy of my 400,000,000 subjects. I would rather be assassinated and have my will made known to the people, than be a prince under a foreign yoke, or have my life saved to serve as a menial, and bear the disgrace of a lost empire. From the time I was made to rule ten years ago, I have secretly been longing all the time for an opportunity to act. I hated the idea of losing Annam. Again, I was indignant at the idea of being shorn of Manchuria and Formosa, and a third time I was indignant at being shorn of Kiaochow and Port Arthur. My mind being full of indignation, I deeply pondered over all the circumstances, and I saw no other course but to risk my life on behalf of the Empire."

The Emperor, in a word, staked everything on reform. Once determined, he acted with vigor and with almost open defiance of the Empress Dowager. He abolished the old examination system, which had been in force since the days of the Sing dynasty, and substituted papers on practical subjects, including a knowledge of the history of other countries and of contemporary politics. He sought to provide for the reorganization of the effete Manchu troops of the metropolitan province and for the founding of colleges and high schools in the provinces to correspond to the University at Peking. More, he arranged for the publication of official gazettes all over the Empire. These gazettes were to be official newspapers, and their object the diffusion of general knowledge. Abuses were to be exposed by their means, and opinions freely expressed, and the Government were to subsidize the organs. Nothing, in fact, would suffice for the long-imprisoned energy of the Emperor. Railway and mining bureaus were to be established in Peking. A Translation Department was inaugurated to publish standard works in foreign languages on Political Economy and Natural Science. The Navy was to be thoroughly overhauled and brought up to date. All that China under the Manchus had despised and rejected, all that China had to learn from Western nations, all that she stood most in need of, was at last to be placed within her reach. And for a moment the reformers dared to hope. But alas! they reckoned without their host. The Old Buddha, when she heard of

these reforms, was *en retraite* at her Summer
Palace. She uttered not one word against
them.

Secretly she expressed her approval of
them to the Emperor, and as secretly organized opposition to them, checkmating the
young enthusiast wherever possible by playing on the prejudices of antiquated officials,
by ridiculing the new plans, and by organizing against them all the vested interests that
they threatened to end for the common good.
The Manchus, alarmed beyond expression at
some of the proposals, besought her to return
and again conduct the Government.

The time was not yet, she told them—they
must wait. At last came a decree abolishing
a number of sinecures and useless Government posts, and the indignation at the Emperor's action rose to boiling-point. He became aware, bitterly aware, of the storm
threatening him, and determined on bold
measures. He realized that so long as the
Empress Dowager remained in the field
against him he would, at the best, find his
policy negatived; at the worst, he would be
supplanted. He determined to seize the Empress Dowager and to kill Jung Lu, her chief
agent and favorite eunuch, who was conspir-
ing against him. It is said that the plan was
overheard by another eunuch, who betrayed

it to the enemy. Who can tell? The Emperor himself, to the day of his death, and on his very death-bed, blamed Yuan-Shi-Kai, with whom he entrusted the arrangements, and who betrayed him instantly to the Empress.

It is urged that the betrayal can, as a matter of policy, be justified: that the Emperor had gone too far, and that the Manchus would have had the Old Buddha back in any case. Perhaps there is a case to be made out in defence of Yuan's action on these lines, though the Reform Party in China have never ceased to execrate the act. In any case it ruined the Emperor. He was seized, imprisoned, and virtually made to abdicate. The Empress Dowager was back on the throne, and the chance of reform from within went by for ever, and with it the last hope of preserving the Manchu dynasty.

V

THE STRUGGLE

THE present reform movement, although simmering for many years, found concrete expression in 1895 by the formation of a " Young China " Party in Canton. Sun Yat Sen was an early adherent, and speedily became a prominent member; a peaceful reform was desired; letters couched in temperate terms were forwarded to the Throne pointing out the serious state of mind of the people, and stating what was required to insure good government. The essence of the movement was the establishment of a form of constitutional government to supplement the corrupt and worn-out system under which China was being ruled. These petitions were taken no notice of for a time. The Government were at the moment engaged in warding off the advance of the Japanese upon Peking, and it was only after the Japanese question was settled that the petitioners for reform were denounced as traitors and their suppression commanded.

It was evident that force would be the only means by which the Manchu rulers could be brought to terms, and as soon as this decision was arrived at men and money were to hand. A large number of disbanded soldiers, after the war with the Japanese, were in Canton. The reformers enlisted these men in their service, and upon a certain day in October, 1895, a plan was arranged for the capture of Canton, and the disposal of the authorities, but without bloodshed if possible. Arms, ammunition, and dynamite were accumulated; soldiers were posted ready to fall upon the city, and a strong force of some four hundred men were to join them from Hong Kong.

The reform committee were assembled on the afternoon of the day before that chosen for the rising, when news came that the intentions of the reformers were discovered. Some of the soldiers fled, others were caught, the committee escaped as best they could; the contingent from Hong Kong were arrested on reaching Canton by steamer, and Sun, after many vicissitudes, reached Macao; thence he proceeded to Hong Kong and left for Honolulu, as related before. Since then several armed risings eventuated. The great desire of the reformers was to obtain possession of an arsenal; the reason being that although they could buy arms, guns, and ammunition, the ammunition was soon exhausted, and there was no ready means of replenishing the store. More than one of the risings collapsed from this cause; and, just when victory was in sight, the news that there was no more ammunition available wherewith to carry on the conflict caused the reformers' army to desist, retreat and disband.

In another carefully planned rising, " Black Flag " troops were collected and assembled in a valley surrounded by a circle of hills, inland from Macao, and within striking distance of Canton; the passes in the hills were seized and held by the rebel soldiers, whose presence was prevented being noised abroad by neither entrance nor exit being allowed to any one. Here the troops awaited their leader and his officers. The officers consisted of trained soldiers from ——— —I may not yet say from whence they came. The contingent of officers, to the number of forty, assembled in Hong Kong, and Sun set out to join them, but to his chagrin and the discomfiture of his plans he was not allowed to land. Whilst on board the boat in Hong Kong harbor, however, he got the news that two of his trusted intimate supporters (his acting secretary and treasurer), travelling by an earlier steamer, had been prevented landing in Hong Kong and taken on to Singapore, where they were arrested and found to have a large sum of money upon them (really the reformers' treasury). Sun had to go on to Singapore, and after long and patient interviews he succeeded in proving that the money was for commercial purposes and got it returned to him. The delay, however, was fatal to the projected expedition.

When Sun returned to Hong Kong he found the officers had departed, that the soldiers were still cooped up in the retreat in the hills, and as he could not join them, being carefully watched, he had instead to send a message to the troops to the effect that they were to march straight across the country and join him out on the coast farther north—a march of many hundreds of miles. These adventurous men did so, brushing aside several attacks upon them, and met Sun at the appointed place on the coast. The troops were then disbanded for the time being, and went away " resolved to meet some other day."

Another military expedition took place from the south, some three years ago, from the Annam border, when the reformers' troops spread over Kwang-si and Kwang-tung provinces and threatened Canton, again in the hopes of gaining possession of an arsenal. Success at first crowned their efforts; the inhabitants welcomed them everywhere, but the same nemesis overtook them, for the ammunition gave out as Canton was just within their grasp.

The last great effort was in 1911. The outbreak occurred at Wu-chang, on the Yangtse river, just above Hankow, with the result we know. The outbreak occurred in consequence of an attempt to disarm the regular troops, a circumstance which requires some explanation. The foreign-drilled troops of China had increased in numbers, in equipment, and efficiency during late years under the able direction of Yuan-Shih-Kai until they numbered, in the beginning of the year 1911, some 130,000 men. That these men were well trained is admitted everywhere, and their courage and efficiency were put to an early test during the Boxer Rising, when they were attacked by the naval contingent of mixed European troops in their attempted march from Tientsin to Peking.

The Chinese soldiers put up so good a fight that the foreign troops had to retire; before superior numbers it is true, but all the foreign officers were impressed with the valor and intelligence with which the Chinese fought. Had the foreign-drilled army continued to be content with Manchu rule, the hopes of the reformers to gain their ends would have been hopeless. Sun Yat Sen's doctrine of freedom had, however, prevailed with the officers even in the highest ranks; and as long as three years ago he was aware that well-nigh half the foreign-drilled army were ready to support his cause, and by January, 1911, three-fourths of the army were pledged to help the reformers. The Government authprities, well informed always, had come to know of the changed temper of the troops, and began to disarm and disband the suspected regiments. This was successfully done at Nanking and elsewhere. At Hankow and Wu-chang two regiments were also disarmed, but a third refused to give up their arms, and the fight began. The rebellion broke out some nine months before the selected date; Sun Yat Sen was abroad in America, much to his chagrin. He could not reach China by way of the Pacific, as he was being carefully watched. So he found his way surreptitiously to New York and thence to London, accompanied by General Homer Lea, the well-known author of " The Valor of Ignorance," who had become so devoted to Sun and his cause that he left his home, although in delicate health, determined to proceed to China and assist in the organization of the reformers' army. Whilst in London Sun saw statesmen, soldiers, sailors, bankers, and other influential men, with results which will be known in the near future. He left London for Paris November 20, 1911. In Singapore he met with an enthusiastic reception from his fellow-countrymen, and more important still, perhaps, his countrywomen. In Hong Kong, forbidden territory to him for many years, he was allowed to land, and proceeded from thence to Shanghai, where again he was afforded a hearty welcome. The Provisional Reform Government set up in Nanking invited him to become their President, a position he at first declined, but ultimately, to the great joy of the people, reluctantly consented to accept. The subsequent doings of this party are common knowledge to-day, and the forbearance, the patriotic spirit in which the temporary Republican Government, under Sun's direction, has conducted affairs has gained the approbation and admiration of the whole world. At the moment of writing Sun has retired from the presidency. Three times did he press upon Yuan-Shih-Kai to take up the position in his stead, and at last succeeded in persuading him to do so. The vice-presidency is announced to have been offered to, and accepted by, General Li-Yuan-Hung. This gallant soldier led the Republican troops to victory after victory in the fighting around Hankow and established their superiority in the field. General Li, by his moderation, his protection of the lives and property of non-combatants, his avoidance of reprisals upon his enemies, as much as by his skilful generalship, has gained universal respect and esteem. Sun's friends and well-wishers, in other words most of the civilized world, are anxiously asking: What about Sun? What is his position to be? To those who know him intimately his behavior is what was expected of him. Self-seeking is foreign to his very nature; publicity plays no part in the life of this extraordinary man. Although he has visited and declared his belief before many audiences in many countries, Sun's desire is, and always has been, to be left out of the picture. He loves his neighbor more than himself, and he puts his country before all.

Sun considers his life's work accomplished, and he leaves his country to be governed, as he himself affirms, by abler hands than his. The acknowledgment of Sun's great work has been tardily admitted by the '' authorities '' and the Press. By some of these his very name was withheld from publication as long as possible, and when mentioned by others it was mostly in terms of something akin to amusement at his presumption. In conversation he was smilingly alluded to as " your troublesome friend." It is to be hoped that Sun's forbearance is for China's good; that it is to his credit all allow; but the future alone can decide the question of whether China will be more ably conducted through her troubles without his presence and control in the councils of the country. That he may be called to high office in the immediate future is more than probable; that he will accept it if his country calls is a foregone conclusion; but it will be necessity and not choice that will induce him to resume the presidency he has just resigned.

The chief reason of Sun Yat Sen being held up to something approaching ridicule by the Legations, the officials of the Imperial Maritime Customs, the Consuls, the Old China hands, and the " authorities " on " things Chinese," who advised the Press in Europe, was that a republic in China was an impossibility, and that any man who could think of such a thing must be a dreamer, a faddist, and a danger to China. When the revolution broke out in November, 1911, the idea that it was serious was ridiculed by those whom the Press consulted in the matter.

These " authorities " stated that a revolution of the kind in China occurred every fifty years, that one was now due, that the present outbreak was merely a " recurring row," and that the men concerned in it, and Sun Yat Sen in particular, were of no importance in the eyes of the Chinese Government, the foreign Legations, the Customs officials, and the bankers, etc., in China. The true reason of this belief was that the representatives of the Press consulted men whose experience of China was confined to Government ways and doings or to the assertions of foreigners in China in touch with officials. Another almost universally stated and credited opinion was that the Chinese, saturated with worship of a throne and respect for its edicts, could never become a republic. Moreover, that they were not ready for a republic, being wholly uneducated in the ways of government. A titular sovereign, a " haloed " being hidden away from them and rendered powerless to rule, was what the Chinese wanted in the opinion of " Old China hands." There has been a being of the kind in China for many a day. The Emperor has been a myth, " a heavenly body " that could not be looked upon, far

less approached. When drawing up the constitution of the College of Medicine in Hong
Kong, and being at the time quite new to
China and the ways of the people, I sug-
gested that Queen Victoria and the Emperor
of China should be asked to be patrons. My
suggestion was received with laughter by my
more experienced colleagues, and I was informed that " I might get Queen Victoria,
but the Emperor of China was a god, and
you would have to write to heaven to get
the Emperor nominated." In the earlier
days my wife and myself used to deprecate
a republic when discussing the matter with
Sun. Living as we do under the sway of a
" crowned democracy," we could imagine no
more perfect form of government, and tried
to persuade Sun to the same.

Many a long discussion was held trying
to turn Sun from his purpose, but gradually,
as years went on, we were persuaded that
a monarchy in China was an impossibility.
Even a titular monarch on the throne meant,
in accordance with Chinese custom, a dowager empress or a mother-in-law at the head
of the house, with attendant eunuchs and all
the environment of princes of the royal clan.
A suggestion that the old Ming dynasty
might be revived Sun was able to cope with.
He had also thought of that; he had per-

sonally investigated the conditions of the descendants of the last Ming Emperor and
found them quiet work-a-day people, earning
their daily bread and totally unfit, as they
were unwilling, to take up the duties of a
throne or ruling a country. " Mending "
the Manchu being impossible, reinstating the
Mings being out of the question, " ending "
the reign of the Manchu completely was the
only alternative. Such being the case, the
one possible form of government left was a
republic, and, contrary to the opinion of both
Chinese and Europeans to commence with,
Sun has convinced his countrymen to his
view.

Not only so, but the few Europeans who
have come into intimate contact with Sun,
and listened to his carefully thought out
judgments, to his well-balanced arguments,
and to his at all times unprejudiced, logical,
and unbiased statements, were driven to the
same conclusion. The Europeans who have
not had the opportunity of hearing the reasoned conclusions of China's great leader
still continued to hanker after an emperor
of a sort, a muzzled monarch who would have
neither part nor power in the government of
the country. These conclusions are scarcely
logical. If the Chinese are capable of con-
ducting the country's affairs without the

Manchu even figuring in the play, why maintain a sovereign and his court, with the inevitable interference of the women and the eunuchs of the royal household? It is said these would be done away with. Well, the eunuchs might be abolished, the women cannot be, and the unfortunate interference of the women around the monarch is as potent to-day as it ever has been in Chinese history. Still is the argument heard that a monarch of a sort is a necessity, and that the Chinese are neither ready nor fitted for a republican form of government. Let us see. China has existed for centuries as a federation of states; a federal form of government has been in existence for at least five hundred years. Of the eighteen provinces of the Middle Kingdom all have been " self-contained "; provincial autonomy well-nigh complete has prevailed to a degree unknown in any republic in existence, and paralleled perhaps only in the relations of the overseas dominions in the British Empire to the Mother Country. Even to the extent of defending the country from foreign foes do the provinces of China maintain their independence. Not once, but many times, have certain provinces in the south and west refused help to the Peking Government.

The Chinese cannot, or could not in the

past, understand the meaning of their country being in danger; an inroad of foreign troops carried with it no meaning of international complications, for to the Chinese there were no other nations; the world outside themselves consisted of subject States and " outer barbarians," and if occasionally these negligible communities gave trouble, it lay with the authorities in the province or provinces where the trouble existed to put it down. How could people far distant from the seat of disturbance be expected to take an active part or interest in matters which did not concern them? The Manchus attempted to maintain the masses of China in ignorance of foreigners and their ways, and succeeded in a marvellous manner in doing so. They dreaded the consequences of the people becoming enlightened, believing that only by keeping them in ignorance would their existence as rulers be tolerated. The adoption of belief in reform methods of government cost the last Emperor his life, and the seal upon ancient methods of preserving ignorance was once more set.

As an example of how ignorant the masses of China were kept by the Manchus, a concrete example will suffice. During the late war with Japan the people in the south of China knew nothing of the trouble. Chi-

nese living in Kowloon—the British territory
on the mainland of China which forms part
and parcel of the colony of Hong Kong—
during the height of the memorable struggle,
not only never heard of the war but they
had never even heard of the Japanese people.
The Government officials in the southern
provinces hesitated to send soldiers or ships
to the north to the aid of their confrères, on
the plea that they (the northerners) had got
into the trouble and they must get out of it
as best they could. There is nothing extraordinary in this declaration to those who know
how independent these provinces are. The
relationship of the Chinese provinces to each
other and to the Throne is paralleled only
within the British Empire. Neither Canada
nor Australia is compelled to take part in a
war in which Great Britain is involved.
During the South African War Cape Colony
remained " neutral " whilst the Mother
Country was preventing the colony being
overrun by the Boers. Independence
is the keynote of the overseas dominions of
Britain to as marked an extent as is that of
the provinces of China to the central
authority.

The provinces of the Middle Kingdom are
merely a federation of states; " Home
Rule " has been their portion; their partici-

pation in any national danger was optional
to a degree. The provinces have been accustomed to govern themselves, and there
need not be, and there will not be, now that a
republican form of government has supplanted a monarchical, any departure from
the " old custom " which has prevailed in
China for centuries.

The many letters which have within the
last few months appeared in the Press from
" authentic " and " authoritative " sources
are amusing reading in the light of to-day.
These letters are still further evidence, if
such were needed, of the " cult " which prevailed in Peking.

In the *Strand Magazine,* under the head-
ing of " My Reminiscences, by Sun Yat
Sen," it is mentioned that Yuan-Shih-Kai
approached Sun some considerable time ago,
and sent a messenger to interview him, and
to convey Yuan's appreciation of what he
was doing, and offering to help him in his
campaign. My wife and myself knew of this
proceeding from Dr. Sun personally, shortly
after its occurrence, but kept the matter a
close secret, believing that it would do infinite harm were the circumstance published
abroad. When Yuan was sent for by the
Manchu Government to get them out of their

troubles, had the fact of his relations with
Sun been told at the time, Yuan would have
been discredited as hunting with both the
hare and the hounds, and his influence would
have been warped, or altogether annihilated.
It was not intended to mention the matter in
this volume at all, considering it a subject
which, with several others told us by Sun,
would do harm " to the cause " if disclosed,
but since this " secret " is published for all
to read in the magazine referred to, there is
no necessity to keep silence in the matter any
longer.

For the immediate future of China the
message sent by Yuan to Sun augurs well.
Yuan was evidently not hide-bound in his
devotion to the Manchus. He had at least
a leaning towards reform, and he must have
a regard for Sun and his principles, otherwise he would not have proffered help. Sun
in his turn has a respect for Yuan, and has
often spoken of his capability and his great
grasp of affairs. With the two great men
in China at the present moment therefore
thinking alike, there is hope for a speedy
coalition and for unanimity in purpose. It
is well that Yuan's leanings towards the reform movement were not known before; now
the publication of the fact can only do good.
Yuan-Shih-Kai has behaved wisely and well,

but in a way which the authorities do not, or at any rate did not, know of.

Had the Manchu Government and foreign representatives been aware of the fact earlier, their attitude would not have been so cordial, and Yuan's name might not have been lauded as it has been. Deserving of all praise Yuan certainly is; but not quite in the way his foreign advocates thought or desired. The power and influence Yuan possesses has been dinned into my ears for many a day—" Yuan is the great power in China, not Sun Yat Sen," and " that troublesome friend of yours is only an agitator that Yuan will soon settle," and similar remarks by wiseacres who knew " all about China." I have been compelled to hear this, knowing all the time that Yuan had approached Sun. I had to be content to hear my friend traduced as a man of no consequence, and as a mere fly to be lightly brushed aside. Yuan was *the* man, but not in the way these " authorities " on " things Chinese " believed. I knew from Sun that Yuan was " sympathetic," and that Sun would stand aside and invite Yuan to become the President of China. A greater man than Yuan was my informant, a man without thought of self, seeking no honor but his country's, regardless of place or power; yet powerful withal, and with a determination that nothing could move from the purpose he had at heart: a patriot in the highest and truest sense of the word; a meek man in all but his country's welfare.

After Sun's release from the Legation in London, 1896, a number of his friends in Canton and Hong Kong sent me a large tablet with Chinese characters inscribed upon it. Several Chinese scholars attempted to interpret the characters, but it was not until Sir James Stewart Lockhart saw the tablet that the full meaning was divulged, when it was found to be a line from the Sermon on the Mount, "Blessed are the merciful." Were I to return the compliment and present a tablet to Sun, I would inscribe upon it a verse preceding the one referred to as interpreting Sun's character: "Blessed are the meek: for they shall inherit the earth." If Sun's principles and men of his disposition and character are to prevail in China, his country shall certainly inherit the earth, and the "yellow peril" will become a reality.

VI

A GRACEFUL TRIBUTE TO THE MINGS —THE REFORM MOVEMENT

A CEREMONY of entrancing interest occurred on February 15, 1912, when Sun Yat Sen, at the time Provisional President of the United Republic of China, proceeded to the sepulchre of Chu Yuan-Chang, the founder of the Ming (Chinese) dynasty, and informed the spirit of the Emperor that the alien Manchu Tartar had been dethroned. The tomb or mausoleum where the first of the Ming Emperors is buried lies just outside Nanking, at that time the capital of the Empire.

An imposing procession visited the tomb, consisting of President Sun Yat Sen, the members of his cabinet, the civic and military officials, and a large escort of soldiers.

The ceremony is interesting in many ways. The fact that the Manchus—the Eastern Tartars as they were formerly styled—were alien usurpers was prominently demonstrated. That Sun Yat Sen was the spokes-

man on the occasion is a circumstance
amounting to a romance, seeing that for fifteen years he has passed through toil and
strife, through dangers innumerable and un-
told hardships, to attain the great object of
his life, namely, the expulsion of the
Manchus.

But most interesting of all points in con-
nection with the dignified and solemn ceremony is the tone and exquisitely beautiful
language in which the prayer and announcement was framed.   The prayer is given in
the *London Times* of April 3, 1912, and although the language loses something by the
fact that it is a translation into English, it
may be safely said the dignity and grandeur
of this prayer has seldom been surpassed in
either ancient or modern literature.   In con-
formity with the Confucian principle of serv-
ing the dead as if they were present in the
flesh, the prayer, conveying information of
the important events in the history of a dynasty, is always communicated to the spirit
tablet of the founder.   The prayer was as
follows:—

" Of old the Sung dynasty became effete,
and the Liao Tartars and Yuen dynasty
Mongols seized the occasion to throw this
domain of China into confusion, to the fierce
indignation of gods and men.   It was then

WORSHIPPING AT THE ANCESTOR'S GRAVE

that Your Majesty, our founder, arose in
your wrath from obscurity, and destroyed
those monsters of iniquity, so that the ancient
glory was won again. In twelve years you
consolidated the Imperial sway, and the dominions of the Great Yü were purged of pol-
lution and cleansed from the noisome Tartar.
Often in history has our noble Chinese race
been enslaved by petty frontier barbarians
from the north. Never have such glorious
triumphs been won over them as Your
Majesty achieved. But your descendants
were degenerate and failed to carry on your
glorious heritage; they entrusted the reins
of government to bad men, and pursued a
short-sighted policy. In this way they encouraged the ambitions of the Eastern Tartar savages, and fostered the growth of their
power. They were thus able to take advantage of the presence of rebels to invade and
possess themselves of your sacred capital.
From a bad eminence of glory basely won,
they lorded it over this most holy soil, and
our beloved China's rivers and hills were
defiled by their corrupting touch, while the
people fell victims to the headsman's axe or
the avenging sword. Although worthy
patriots and faithful subjects of your dynasty crossed the mountain ranges into Canton and the far south, in the hope of re-

deeming the glorious Ming tradition from utter ruin, and of prolonging a thread of the old dynasty's life, although men gladly perished one after the other in the forlorn attempt, Heaven's wrath remained unappeased, and mortal designs failed to achieve success. A brief and melancholy page was added to the history of your dynasty, and that was all.

"As time went on, the law became ever harsher, and the meshes of its inexorable net grew closer. Alas for our Chinese people, who crouched in corners and listened with startled ears, deprived of power of utterance, and with tongues glued to their mouths, for their lives were past saving. Those others usurped titles to fictitious clemency and justice, while prostituting the sacred doctrines of the sages: whom they affected to honor. They stifled public opinion in the Empire in order to force acquiescence in their tyranny. The Manchu despotism became so thorough and so embracing that they were enabled to prolong their dynasty's existence by cunning wiles. But even so, rebellions occurred. In Yung Cheng's reign the Hunanese Chang Hsi and Tseng Ching preached sedition against the dynasty in their native province, while in Chia Ching's reign the Palace conspiracy of Lin Ching dismayed that monarch in his

capital. These events were followed by rebellions in Sze-chuan and Shensi: under Tao-
Kuang and his successor the Taipings started
their campaign from a remote Kwangsi village. Although these worthy causes were
destined to ultimate defeat, the gradual
trend of the national will became manifest.
At last our own era dawned, the sun of freedom had risen, and a sense of the rights of
the race animated men's minds. In addition
the Manchu bandits could not even protect
themselves. Powerful foes encroached upon
the territory of China, and the dynasty
parted with our sacred soil to enrich neigh-
boring nations. The Chinese race of to-day
may be degenerate, but it is descended from
mighty men of old. How should it endure
that the spirits of the great dead should be
insulted by the everlasting visitation of this
scourge?

"Then did patriots arise like a whirlwind or like a cloud which is suddenly manifested in the firmament. They began with
the Canton insurrection; then Peking was
alarmed by Wu Yüeh's bomb (in 1905). A
year later Hsu Hsilin fired his bullet into the
vitals of the Manchu robber chief, En Ming,
Governor of Anhui. Hsiung Chêng-chi
raised the standard of liberty on the Yang-
tse's banks; rising followed rising all over

the Empire, until the secret plot against the Regent was discovered, and the abortive insurrection in Canton startled the capital. One failure followed another, but other brave men took the place of the heroes who died, and the Empire was born again to life. The bandit Manchu Court was shaken with pallid terror, until the cicada shook off its shell in a glorious regeneration, and the present crowning triumph was achieved. The patriotic crusade started in Wuchang; the four corners of the Empire responded to the call. Coast regions nobly followed in their wake, and the Yang-tse was won back by our armies. The region south of the Yellow River was lost to the Manchus, and the north manifested its sympathy with our cause. An earthquake shook the barbarian Court of Peking, and it was smitten with a paralysis. To-day it has at last restored the Government to the Chinese people, and the five races of China may dwell together in peace and mutual trust. Let us joyfully give thanks. How could we have attained this measure of victory had not Your Majesty's soul in heaven bestowed upon us your protecting influence?

" I have heard say that triumphs of Tartar savages over our China were destined never to last longer than a hundred years. But

the reign of these Manchus endured unto
double, aye, unto treble, that period. Yet
Providence knows the appointed hour, and
the moment comes at last. We are initiating
the example to Eastern Asia of a Republican
form of government; success comes early or
late to those who strive, but the good are
surely rewarded in the end. Why then
should we repine to-day that victory has
tarried long?

"I have heard that in the past many
would-be deliverers of their country have
ascended this lofty mound wherein is your
sepulchre. It has served to them as a holy
inspiration. As they looked down upon the
surrounding rivers and upward to the hills,
under an alien sway, they wept in the bitter-
ness of their hearts, but to-day their sorrow
is turned into joy. The spiritual influences
of your grave at Nanking have come once
more into their own. The dragon crouches
in majesty as of old, and the tiger surveys
his domain and his ancient capital. Everywhere a beautiful repose doth reign. Your
legions line the approaches to the sepulchre:
a noble host stands expectant. Your people
have come here to-day to inform Your
Majesty of the final victory. May this lofty
shrine wherein you rest gain fresh lustre
from to-day's event and may your example

inspire your descendants in the times which
are to come. Spirit! Accept this offering!"

Perhaps nothing will strike the historian,
who undertakes to write an account of the
Reform Movement in China of 1911-12, more
forcibly than the extraordinary care and the
scientific acumen with which the foundations
of the Republic were laid. Different from
every other revolution we know of, that
which we have just seen completed in China
was not the result of an imbroglio, a mere
whirlwind of passion, nor yet the outcome
of a mob rising; even the fighting has been
but a small part of the revolutionary movement—a side-issue which in every way possible it was hoped and intended to avoid.
For fifteen years Sun had been organizing
the great movement, and striving to place it
upon a firm basis. How did he do it? By
preparing men for the government of the
country under the new *régime*. Ten years
ago the Reform Party sent the most promising Chinese students in the country to be
educated abroad, so that they might be able
to fill important positions in the cabinet and
in the various departments of government.
In Europe and America several hundreds of
young Chinese were engaged in studies of
all kinds, with a view to becoming legislators

and councillors. The men were being trained whilst yet the Manchus ruled and their hold on the throne seemed secure.

A preparation for occupying positions which did not, and in the minds of many would never, exist, would strike most men as the product of a fantastic brain, and as the mere dreams of an idealist. First create the positions and then find the men is the usual method adopted in undertakings of the kind. When the revolution has been success- ful it will be surely time enough then to think of men to fill the vacant posts, is the short- sighted plan of the empiricist. Not so in Sun's idea. He took advantage of the men sent abroad by the late Emperor, whilst yet he held the reins of government, to be trained in modern methods of education and govern- ment, and in addition to these the Reform Party supplemented the number by nominees of their own. During his visits to Europe and America Sun saw these men, conferred with them, and took them into his counsels. That he was held in their high esteem was evi- dent from the fact that whilst in Brussels (or some other European capital) many of the students in the different parts of Europe came to meet him on the several occasions of his visits. The proof that they actually did meet Sun is testified by the evidence of photographs in my possession, in which, amongst a group of Chinese students, Sun is given the place of honor in the centre, and as a rule is seated whilst the others stand around him. These men represent modern China to-day; they were chosen for training abroad from amongst the best men to be found, and some of them are members of the oldest and best families. Yuan-Shih-Kai, when he made up his cabinet, said that it was composed of the best men China possessed, and it is a fact that the highest positions were given by Yuan to Sun's foreign-educated *protégés*.

It will be remembered also that many of these men nominated by Yuan to serve in his cabinet refused to take up office under him, and joined Sun's cabinet in Nanking, so that, according even to Yuan's testimony, China's ablest men were in Sun's cabinet. The most recent published list of ministers is dated Peking, March 30, 1912, and reads as follows:—

Premier and Minister of Communications, ad interim: TANGSHAOYI.

Minister for Foreign Affairs: LU-CHENG-HSIAN, hitherto Chinese Minister in St. Petersburg.

Minister of Interior: CHAO-PING-CHUN, who is reappointed.

Minister of Finance: HSUING-HSI-LING, a financier of moderate ability who has espoused the revolutionary cause.

Minister of War: GENERAL TUAN-CHI-JUI, formerly Viceroy of Hukuang.

Minister of Marine: LIU-KUAN-HSUNG (Progressive.)

Minister of Education: TSAI-YUAN-PEI, leader of the Southern delegates, a Progressive educationist.

Minister of Justice: WANG-TSUNG-HUI.

Minister of Agriculture: SUN-KHIA-JEN.

(The two last named were comparatively unknown before the outbreak of the revolution.)

Minister of Commerce: CHEN-CHI-MEI, a prominent Shanghai revolutionary.

HIN-YUN GUIDE US.

THE CHINESE SONG IN TIME OF REVOLUTION.

FREEDOM, one of the greatest blessings of Heaven.
United to Peace thou wilt work on this earth
Ten thousand wonderful new things.
Grave as a spirit, great as a giant
Rising to the very skies,
With the clouds for a chariot and the wind for a
    steed,
Come, come to reign over the earth.
For the sake of the black hell of our slavery,
Come, enlighten us with a ray of thy sun.

White Europe. Thou art indeed
The spoiled daughter of Heaven.

Bread, wine—thou hast everything in abundance.
For me, I love Liberty as a bride.
Through the day in my thoughts, through the
    night in my dreams
I survey the woes of my fatherland.
But the inconstant nature of Liberty
Prevents me from attaining her.
Alas, my brethren are all slaves.

The wind is so sweet, the dew is so bright,
The flowers are so fragrant,
Men are becoming all kings—
And yet can we forget what the people are
    suffering?
At Peking we must bow our head
Before the wolf of an Emperor.
Alas, Freedom is dead.
Asia the Great is nothing else
But an immense desert.

In this century we are working
To open a new age.
In this century, with one voice, all virile men
Are calling for a new making of heaven and
    earth.
May the soul of the people rise to the peak of
    Kwang-tung.
Washington and Napoleon, you two sons of
    Liberty,
May you become incarnated in the people.
Hin-yun, our ancestor, guide us.
Spirit of Freedom, come and protect us.

VII

THE FLAG OF THE NEW REPUBLIC

THE five stripes on the Republican flag of China bring home to us the fact that the Chinese Empire is a congeries of peoples of Mongoloid type. The Chinese have for so long a period been the predominant section of the Mongolian race that the terms Mongol and Chinese have come to be regarded as well-nigh synonymous. So much so has this been the case that the Mongolian invasion of Western Asia and Eastern Europe is often termed a Chinese invasion, whereas it was at least directed by the Mongolians or Western Tartars, as the Chinese describe them. The ambition of all princes and khans of the Mongolian race was to gain possession of the throne of the Middle Kingdom. This was accomplished first by the Mongolian or Western Tartars and subsequently by the Manchurian or Eastern Tartars. The conquerors, however, became incorporated with the Middle Kingdom, and their countrymen were spoken of subse-

quently as Chinese. No other empiré quite
corresponds to that of China, the nearest
approach to it being the British, but in China
the several dominions are coterminous,
whereas the British Empire is widely flung
over seas.

The five component factors in the flag represent (1) The Chinese of the eighteen home
provinces, constituting the Middle Kingdom
—or China proper. (2) The Manchurian
people, styled the Eastern Tartars by the
Chinese, who occupy the district of Manchuria, their ancient kingdom. (3) The
Mongolians, the Western Tartars, who have
from time to time proved so important an
element in the destinies of China. (4) The
Thibetans, a remote people upon whom the
hold of China has been lax at times and again
reasserted. (5) The Mahommedans who, although possessing no nationality, are a powerful religious sect within the widespread
domains. To understand aright the part
played by each of the groups represented
within the flag would involve an intimate
knowledge of Chinese history, which would
be beyond the purpose of this sketch. However, seeing that China will now occupy a
more prominent place in modern history, a
few notes are appended on the subject.

    1. The red or upper stripe in the Repub-

THE NATIONAL FLAG OF THE CHINESE REPUBLIC.

In the Flag five colours are arranged in parallel stripes; these serve to indicate the several component elements of the Republic.

From above downwards they are:—

Red—Middle Kingdom, China Proper.
Yellow—The Manchurians or Eastern Tartars.
Blue—The Mongolian or Western Tartars.
White—The Thibetans.
Black—The Mohammedans.

lican flag denotes the Chinese—the inhabitants of the Middle Kingdom, the predominant Mongol people.

It is impossible to ascertain the origin of the Chinese from recorded history. The race at present dwelling in the Middle Kingdom are believed to have originated near the supposed cradle of the human race in that indefinite area associated with the name of Mesopotamia. A nomad people, they travelled northeastward, carrying with them ideas of settled government, a knowledge of agriculture, of the production of silk, and the value and use of the mulberry-tree. This blackhaired race, as their neighbors styled them, found what we now call the Chinese Empire inhabited by " fiery dogs " in the north, " great bowmen " in the east, " mounted warriors " in the west, and " ungovernable vermin " in the south. The types remain fairly well represented to-day: the fiery Tartar to the north, Manchurian bowmen to the eastward, Mongolian horsemen to the west, and to the south the clever inhabitants of the Kwang-tung (Canton), Kwangsi, and Fokien provinces.

Amongst the yellow race, the Chinese, as distinct from Mongols, Tartars, etc., have preserved their intellectual, commercial, and political superiority, and are therefore entitled to have their nationality represented as the premier power in the federation.

2. The second color in the flag—yellow—represents the Manchurian or Eastern Tartars, as they were formerly styled.

The Manchu dynasty, which has occupied the throne since the year 1643, deserves the second place in the Empire for more reasons than one.

The inroads of the Eastern and Western Tartars (Mongols and Manchus) had long been a trouble and danger to the Chinese. The Great Wall of China was built two thousand years ago to keep them out. Extending over hill and dale for 1,500 miles inland, from the point where it touches the seacoast at Shan-hai-Kwan on the shores of the Gulf of Pechili, this stupendous structure, the greatest monument to labor ever accomplished, may be termed "China's folly," just as the Yellow River is styled "China's sorrow," and serves to show the dread with which these Tartar hordes were regarded. It is jokingly said the expense entailed in the building of this wall was such that the Chinese never got over it, but the Tartars did. When the wall failed in its purpose bribes, concessions, and payments in cash were tried instead, but the Eastern Tartars (Manchus) reduced the northern portion of China to

SUN YAT SEN, WHILE PRESIDENT OF THE REPUBLIC, BEING SALUTED BY SOLDIERS

vassalage and were in a position to seize the throne. This they were prevented doing by the advance of the Western Tartars (Mongols) under the famous Kublai Khan, who not only drove out the Eastern Tartars (Manchus) but seized the country and styled themselves Emperors of China. Kublai Khan, the first of the Yuen dynasty, favored Buddhism, which has never flourished in China as it did under the Mongol Tartar rule. Peking, originally a Tartar encampment, was designated the capital. Gradually, however, luxurious living developed effeminacy amongst the Tartars, and so effete did they become that in A.D. 1366 the Chinese drove them from the throne and founded the Ming or Chinese dynasty.

The Mings, as seemed to be the case with every succeeding dynasty in China, gradually became so effete that they at last drove their own Chinese countrymen into revolt. The leader of the rebellion was so successful that in 1643 he invested Peking, and rather than submit to capture the last of the Ming Emperors committed suicide. All China seemed at the feet of the rebel leader, the only force in existence loyal to the Mings being an army near to the Manchurian border; and they were reduced to such straits that they invoked the aid of the Eastern Tartars

(Manchus), who readily accepted the invitation, and after defeating the Chinese rebels, the Manchu king entered Peking and seized the throne. Thus did the Manchus or Eastern Tartars enter China and assume the sovereignty, which they held until 1912, when a republic was declared with Dr. Sun Yat Sen as the first President.

3. The third or blue color in the flag represents the Western Tartars or Mongolians. The color is reminiscent of the " blue wolf," from which the Mongol sovereigns are mythically held to be " descended." The Mongolians had long been a trouble to the Middle Kingdom folk, and their audacity culminated when, under the greatest soldier of his day, Kublai Khan, they invaded the country and established their rule at Peking. However, in the short period of eighty years Kublai Khan's descendants had to flee the country and seek refuge amongst the Eastern Tartars (Manchus), where they intermarried with the ruling family, so that the Manchu princes claim to have the blood of the Mongolian Emperors in their veins.

4. Thibet is represented in the Republican flag as the fourth section of the State by the white stripe. The tenacity with which China has adhered to the possession of the barren region of Thibet may be ascribed

largely to the fact that the Grand Lama resides at Lhassa, the Rome and Mecca of China in a religious sense.

Buddhism is tolerated in China, as are all other religions which do not interfere with the State religion of Confucianism. Five religions at least have their followers in China—Confucianism (the State religion), Buddhism, Taoism, Mahommedanism, and Christianity. It may be safely said all Chinese are primarily Confucians. Buddhism has no hold on the people; it is confined almost entirely to an exercise of ritual practised in temples and monasteries by priests. The language in which the form of worship is conducted is that of a bastard Hindustani, which is not only not understood by the Chinese, but even the priests who perform the ceremonies are for the most part wholly ignorant of the meaning of the words they use. The words are, in fact, mere sounds which convey nothing to either priest or worshippers.

Taoism, a religion of reason, has degenerated from the ideals originally given it by Tao, the founder. This philosopher, who taught about the same time as Confucius, preached and practised a doctrine of inactivity, a neglect of the world and its concerns, loving neither fame, pleasure, nor business.

At present, however, the professed Taoists are for the most part jugglers and necromancers, who claim intimate relationship with demons. In some temples are found effigies of " the three pure ones," indicating a Triad fraternity—an imitation, no doubt, of the Buddhist Triad. Alchemy, a search for the elixir of longevity, magic, and a form of the healing art of the nature of the Christian Science of to-day, are traits of Taoism which now are followed only by the most ignorant of the people.

5. The Mahommedans within the Chinese Empire are represented by the black stripe in the Republican flag. In their wide range of conquests the Mongols overcame many Mahommedan peoples, and their conquests—more especially in Syria and in Baghdad, where Genghis Khan overthrew the famous Caliphate—brought them into close contact with Mahommedanism. Many diverse sects, tribes and communities are scattered throughout the Chinese Empire, and even within the Middle Kingdom itself Mahommedans are found who represent some of the most warlike of its peoples.

Christians are not represented in the Republican flag, although ever since the first century of the Christian era Christianity has found supporters now with the Mongol rulers, now with the Chinese Emperors, and many of the people of both countries have followed its tenets. Nestorians carried the Gospel to the Far East and incorporated many of its doctrines into several forms of worship in Central Asia and China. Jesuits and Dominican priests found favor with the Emperors in Peking for several centuries, but when it was found out that the Pope and not the Emperor was the controlling agent in directing religious affairs, Roman Catholicism fell into disfavor, being renounced by the governing class, whilst many of its adherents were killed. Of late years many sections of the Christian Church have sent missionaries to China, and so long as they do not interfere with the political affairs of the country as the Jesuits did, so long will they be allowed to preach the Gospel and to found churches. It is significant that the Taiping Rebellion, although headed by Christians, was put down by the help of Christian nations, and the first President of the Republic of China, Sun Yat Sen, is a Christian by birth, education, and profession. The tolerance of all forms of religious belief in China is a tribute to the broadmindedness of the Chinese, and that form of Christianity will succeed which is based upon the will of the people and refrains from attempting to interfere with the philosophic teaching of Confucius, the State religion (so-called) of China.

The Christians, although fairly numerous, are scattered throughout the land, and their influence in the history of China is not deemed worthy of a stripe in the national flag, a fact perhaps all in favor of future success.

A Chinaman may be a Confucian and yet a sound Christian, Buddhist, Taoist, or Mahommedan. Confucianism is a philosophy, not a religion, and its acceptance no more hinders a Chinese being a Christian than does a belief in Darwinism prohibit an Englishman being a devout Churchman.

VIII

THINGS CHINESE

TO attempt a history of China, even to give an outline of an empire founded and its people civilized before Greece rose to eminence or Rome was heard of, would be the task of a lifetime. All that can be attempted is to state a few, a very few, of the more prominent characteristics of this extraordinary people, their everyday beliefs and ways.

Five thousand years ago at least the civilization of the Chinese was in an extraordinary state of advance; in fact, they were perhaps the people of all mankind to be earliest civilized, and their records would seem to stamp them at that time as possibly but little different from the Chinese of to-day. When the Mongols entered Eastern Europe they found a barbarous people, and the legend " Outer Barbarian " remains with them as a term for Europeans to this day in consequence.

There is the account of the people of what

is now the city of Dresden, when the Chinese
garrison was about to be withdrawn, petition-
ing the authorities to allow the Chinese governor to remain, inasmuch as they had never
been so well governed. This Chinese was,
perhaps, the most highly civilized man and
possibly the first trained official they had ever
seen, and they were anxious for him to stay.
Should he leave they dreaded a relapse to the
old " barbaric " *régime* of government again.
Marco Polo, although in the history of China
the visits of this traveller are but as yesterday, found difficulty not when he had entered
China, but in the countries he had to traverse
to reach the Chinese boundary. Once in Chinese territory he found magnificent roads,
with inns and posting establishments at every
thirty miles' interval on his way from the
Caspian to the capital of China. Order
reigned wherever the Chinese ruled and settled government prevailed. Their literature,
their agriculture, their medical knowledge,
and several industries such as that of silk,
were in an advanced state before Moses was
cradled or Solomon built his temple.

We may well be asked why they have not
continued to advance. The reply may be
summed up as isolation due perhaps for the
most part to natural forces. The relapse of
Central Asia into a desert formed a barrier

THE "FU-TSI-MIAO,"
or Confucian Temple at Nanking

BUDDHIST TEMPLE ON ISLAND OF PU-TI,
The most sacred place in Chinese Buddhism

between China and Western Asia which it
was quite impossible to contend with. The
desert has gradually encroached, and is still
encroaching, upon the western frontiers of
China. The desiccation of Central Asia has
obliterated many fertile lands, and it is only
a process of time until the capital shares a
similar fate. The sand is gradually encroaching on Peking, and this should prove an additional reason for removing the capital from
Peking to Nanking. Southward advance into
India was thwarted by the Himalayas, for
mountains then, as now, present the greatest
difficulties to be overcome by armies; they
constitute the chief barriers also to the inter-
community of peoples, and debar effective
military occupations of remote territories.
When China became separated from the
West, her people, hemmed in by mountains
and cut off by impassable deserts, lost touch
with the rest of mankind, with the result
that they relapsed into a state of inborn con-
ceit, which led them to imagine that they were
the people, and that the rest of the world
remained as they had originally found them,
in a state of " utter barbarism." It was only
when ships of sufficient size were built by
Europeans to travel long distances that
China was again brought into contact with
the outer world. For about five hundred

years at least they had been left to themselves, and it was not until the Portuguese,
some three hundred and fifty years ago, followed by the Dutch and the English, reached
China by sea, that the Chinese had any
knowledge of the change which had occurred
amongst the inhabitants of Europe. For
some three centuries they held these visitors
in contempt and reluctantly tolerated them
at only a few of their ports. They took no
heed of these men who came thither in
their ships to barter goods for tea and
silk.

Gradually, however, the trade increased;
the visits of these unwelcome " foreign devils " were tolerated at times, and again
thwarted by edicts promulgated by the Manchu rulers. One says the Manchu rulers ad-
visedly; for before the Manchu *régime,* whilst
China was governed by the Ming (or Chinese) Emperors, foreigners were allowed to
enter and travel through the country unmo-
lested. As the British traders became more
and more persistent in their attempts to open
up trade in tea and silk, troubles arose which
led to several wars during the last century,
with the result that treaties and concessions
were insisted upon and some ports were
opened at which trade with the foreigner was
allowed.

Thus gradually has China been made cognizant of the civilization of the West, with the consequences we know of to-day, when the people have been aroused from their lethargy under the stimulating influence of Sun and his colleagues. Had China had no tea or silk to sell, she would have been left alone much longer; there would have been no inducement for the European to make the long voyages, which in the days of sailing-ships extended to more than a year, from Britain to China and back. In this manner has China passed through the phases of her development—a change brought about by a natural sequence of events partly geographical, partly owing to the demand for the products which she was alone able to supply to the rest of the world.

The armies of the Chinese Empire in earlier times penetrated far beyond the immediate confines of their home territories and compelled submission and demanded tribute from many tribes and potentates. Their advance across Western Asia and their presence in Eastern Europe came nigh to swamp the Eurasian continents and establish a Mongoloid in place of an Indo-European people in Europe and South-West Asia. They left their mark in Russia, and the phrase " Scratch a Russian and you will find a Tar-

tar " holds good to-day. Southward the
Mongolians crossed the Himalayas and left
the Nepalese—a Mongolian people—as a leg-
acy. They passed into Burmah and peopled
it. Siam, Annam, Cochin China, and Cam-
bodia had to bow before their might, and to
the present time most of these countries pay
tribute to China. The tribute may be nothing more than a bowl of rice, a present of
flowers, a mere " pepper-corn " tribute, but
still it is " tribute," and neglect to forward
it is regarded as a slight to the suzerain and
a punishable offence. Asia and half Europe,
in the days of Genghis Khan and Kublai
Khan, were practically at their feet, and they
believed there were no more " worlds " to
conquer. Satiated with conquest, having obtained the mastery of all around them, possessing a civilization as superior in its form
to their neighbors' as ours is to-day to that
of the court of Dahomey, it is scarcely to be
wondered at that they grew conceited and
wrapped themselves up in self-satisfaction.
Arms could achieve no more, and they came
to regard prowess on the field of battle an
unworthy calling for intellectual men to
follow.

With the world as they knew it paying
tribute, arms and armies seemed uncalled
for; their advanced civilization reached the

stage which some Western Europeans wish
to see attained at the present day, namely,
the abolition of armies in favor of international courts of justice, where all matters
in dispute between nations are to be adjudi-
cated. The Chinese attained this pinnacle of
super-civilization five hundred years ago.
The status of the soldier was depreciated and
regarded as a caste and calling of a low,
perhaps the lowest, degree. Only now is
Western Europe dreaming of such a state of
civilization; the Chinese not only dreamt of
it but acted upon it, and it has proved their
undoing. Super-civilization of the kind is
theoretically beautiful in its conception, and
would, no doubt, be possible of attainment
if there existed but one ruler or one predominant race in the world. The Chinese,
so far as they knew the world, were in that
position and could afford to convert their
swords into pruning-hooks. Unfortunately
for the fulfilment of their dream of peace,
there appeared barbarians from the outer
world, who desired not only commercial relationship, but who had the presumption to
present petitions to the Throne, and refused
to allow their people to be judged or punished according to the law of China. This
led to trouble, to war, to loss of territory, to
humiliation, and to " loss of face " in the

eyes of the world and in their estimation of themselves.

China had no armed force wherewith to withstand the inroads of these " outer barbarians "; militarism as a profession was held in contempt, and not all the edicts of the " Son of Heaven " could drive the barbarians back to their dens. It might be thought, and with a high degree of reason, that a nation to whom fighting was abhorrent and regarded as degrading would, in the course of some five hundred years, find the fighting instincts of the people blunted, and that the men would have become effete and would shrink from war and battle.

In this condition of unalloyed peace, the result of military prowess, China might have continued indefinitely had she been left alone. But it was not to be. The almost complete isolation that had so long prevailed became impossible as new modes of travel both by sea and land developed. Foreigners came to Chinese shores first in their large ocean-going sailing-ships, attracted thither by the desire for the tea, silk, camphor, &c., which the Chinese produced and because they found a ready market for rice, sugar, cotton goods, and the thousand-and-one articles which go to make up the merchandise of

" necessaries." Not to be put off, foreigners approached from all sides.

In the north and west the Russians and Central Asian peoples closed in upon the frontiers of the Middle Kingdom. The seaports were visited by Europeans, and concessions demanded at the point of the bayonet, which was occasionally thrust home. The establishment of foreign embassies and consulates was insisted upon, treaties were enforced at the cannon's mouth, and of late years territory has been seized and held by several Powers. The Chinese have, in fact, been driven by force into becoming a mere *nation,* whilst a century ago they were a dominant *people.* The elephant amongst nations, China has been pestered, worried, and nibbled at by the rest of the world until she has come to realize that her sway is not universal, that her boundaries are not illimitable, and that she cannot nowadays compel world-wide tribute. At first she regarded the visits of these foreigners as a passing phenomenon in her existence that would soon cease; the people who came to her shores claiming to be civilized she had formerly known only as barbarians; compared with China these modern nations were regarded as creations of yesterday and of mushroom growth—mere froth, which would bubble for

a while and then fade away into the ocean
from whence it came.

It is the interference of the foreign Powers
that has made China a nation, and for the
first time for many centuries she has had to
buckle to and see to it that her frontiers
are respected, that her power is established,
and that her house is put in order. That
she can do it is beyond doubt, and that she
will do it the Chinese themselves are determined upon. Let the nations who have
brought this about look to themselves. These
are no barbarous people emerging into the
refulgence of an unaccustomed civilization,
but a people of high and ancient civilization
being narrowed down to become a nation.
Resourceful, capable, and self-reliant, the
Chinese possess all the qualities and attributes of greatness. It is said there are three
elements necessary to make a people great—
prowess in the field, diplomatic ability, and
commercial instincts. China has had, and
still has, all three and some of them in a
superlative degree. The first of these has
been in abeyance for some centuries but the
fighting instinct is there, and it wants but
to be organized to place it on a level of
excellence with the others.

The efficiency and superiority of the armies
of China reached a maximum of attainment

in the days of Genghis Khan and Kublai Khan. These great soldiers reduced well-nigh all Asia to submission and conquered in Europe wherever they appeared. So firmly was the military superiority of China established, that its very thoroughness proved the undoing of the country, for, satiated with success, soldiering came to be neglected, and organized armies passed out of existence. No foemen worthy of their steel were left, the sword was condemned to rust, and the nation gave itself over to literature (unfortunately of a useless kind) and to commerce. The Emperors ruled the nation and kept the people in submission and in darkness by a few regiments, and the fighting instinct of the people was curbed and scotched. That it was not destroyed, however, recent events have shown, and its continued existence has proved the salvation of the country. Without it there would have been no reform achieved; the Manchus would have continued their harassing rule and kept the people of China in ignorance and backwardness.

As examples of fortitude in the field we have several modern instances. Take, for example, Gordon's testimony during the Taiping Rebellion of the courage displayed by the men in the " Ever Victorious " Army.

Not only did Gordon's men earn encomiums from their leader, but their Taiping adversaries fought with a determination which won the admiration of the foreign officers who served in Gordon's army.

Again, during the recent Boxer Rising the officers of the allied European armies accorded a high meed of praise to the capability and bravery of the Chinese troops opposed to them, and on one memorable occasion at least the allies had to retire before their adversaries. In the recent fighting also around Hankow a British surgeon relates how keen the Chinese soldiers were. Seriously wounded men, after their wounds were dressed, could with difficulty be restrained from returning to the fighting line; even when so severely injured as to require to be taken to hospital, it was no uncommon thing to find on visiting the hospital in the morning that wounded soldiers had escaped during the night and again gone to the front. That they did so was confirmed by the fact that several of the previously wounded men were brought again to hospital suffering from further wounds which totally incapacitated them.

This is evidence of valor worthy of the bravest; and affords abundant testimony that the fighting instincts and courage of the Chinese have not been lost.

Along with the courage and readiness to fight, the Chinese have occasionally resorted to tactics now Fabian, now Machiavellian in their type. Sometimes devices showing supreme genius characterized their efforts in dealing with an enemy; examples of which there are many. As an instance of the kind, and at the same time showing how well the Chinese could be kept in hand when necessity demanded, the story of a rebel leader will serve to illustrate. The supremacy of the Manchu rulers was not universally received throughout China when, in A.D. 1643, they ascended the throne.

Many Chinese refused to shave their heads in token of submission and to adopt the Tartar fashion of a long plaited tress or cue. A portion of the south remained unsubdued, and under a maritime leader, Koshinga, remained true to the Chinese, or Ming dynasty, cause. Co-operating with adherents on shore, Koshinga, with his headquarters on the island of Formosa, not only enlisted the Chinese fleet, but he also got together the boat population of Formosa and of the China coast, and led a predatory host to plunder and sack one city after another along the Chinese littoral. He swept over Canton,

Amoy, Swatow, Foochow, Shanghai, &c., and
no place adjacent to the sea or the estuaries
of rivers was safe from his onslaught. The
authorities on the mainland were helpless;
they had no boats wherewith to attack, for
every fisherman, sailor and pirate with their
crafts had joined the rebels; there were not
sufficient troops in the country to garrison
the towns along 2,500 miles of sea-coast, and
no warning was ascertainable as to where
the next attack was to be made. For years
did this continue, and the authorities were
driven to despair. At last a plan of campaign was devised which for ingenuity of
conception and enormity of detail has no
parallel. It was no other than that the entire population of the sea-coasts of China
should retire inland, leaving the towns and
country bare. Not only did the people move
away from the shore, but animals of every
kind were removed; houses were emptied of
their effects; provender that could not be
carried inwards was destroyed, and the country for three leagues from the sea was
rendered a desert. When next the rebel
fleet attacked there was nothing to be
obtained.

One city after another told the same tale,
until at last want of supplies began to have
its effect; the rough adherents began to quar-

rel amongst themselves; the scramble for food
became severe, and the delinquents reverted
to the Emperor. Finally the instigator of
the rebellion was compelled to deliver Formosa to the Government, and peace was restored. A nation capable of devising and
carrying out so gigantic a co-ordination of
the masses—for some 30,000,000 of people
were affected by the removal—is a dangerous
one to encounter.

Again, the extraordinary persistency and
patience whereby an invading army from
Turkestan was driven back for some 700
miles across the desert district of Chinese
Tartary by the " agricultural army " in the
middle of last century showed a power of
resource and a genius of a kind peculiarly
Chinese. Unable to meet the enemy in an
open engagement, the Chinese troops, under
the crafty Tso-Tsun-Tau, encamped in the
neighborhood of the opposing force and held
a piece of ground which they cultivated, and
on it grew their food. Now they would
harass their opponents and cut off their supplies, and so compel them to retire a certain
distance. The Chinese again followed them
up, cultivated the ground and had plenty of
food, whilst their enemy was almost starved,
or lived upon the victuals the Chinese chose
to sell them. Now the Chinese soldiers

would actually appear in the enemy's camp selling food of all kinds which they had cultivated, and at the same time obtain knowledge of the numbers and disposition of the enemy's forces. Then they would withhold supplies, again loot convoys, and reduce the enemy to the verge of starvation, and thus compel another retirement. Again the Chinese would follow them at a safe distance. These tactics were repeated time after time until the invaded territory was recovered and incorporated once more in the Empire. An enemy possessing so high a degree of patience and fertility of resource is a troublesome one to meet in conflict.

War, however, we have seen, became a despicable thing to the super-civilized Chinese, and the way in which they latterly regarded their god of war was in consonance with this attitude of mind. Every feature of life in China and every occupation has its presiding deity. Each god has to be propitiated, but whilst lip service or physical homage is given him the respect for his omnipotence is really but scant. The god of war is supposed to watch over not only the chances of war, but the munitions of warfare; the guns, the shot and shell, and even the efficacy of charges of gunpowder are under his protection and in his hands.

A GATE OF PEKING

One of the sixteen double gates in the outer wall

Yet do the people, under the war god's "very nose," as it were, steal the gunpowder and fill the vacancy with sand or sawdust; cannon-shot is removed bodily, utilized for making implements, and its place taken by lumps of clay, shaped and painted to look like metal shot; the mountings are stolen from the gun carriages, so that the guns are thereby rendered useless. Even the very guns themselves are at times removed, as the following account shows: When travelling to Peking in 1894, on horseback from Tientsin, as we approached Peking, the forts in the walls loomed large and threatening. Addressing the Chinese guide, I remarked that there was no fear of the Russians getting into Peking with all these guns in the forts. "Oh, no," laconically remarked the guide. After a time he said: "They no belong proper guns" ("These are not proper guns"). "Oh! what is the matter with them? They look all right." "No," he remarked, "You look see, have makee paint 'em guns." I again looked, and could see the mouths of many guns in the embrasures. My further interrogations led to the statement, "Have steal 'em gun, what thing you see belong piecee wood." Sure enough it was so. The guns had been removed, pieces of wood filled the embrasures, and a gun-mouth was carefully and exactly painted on the wood.

I remarked that it was very foolish to do this, " What for makee fool pidgeon all the same? " (" Why do you condescend to such foolish business? "). " Oh," said the guide, " that war god he belong number one fooloo; he thinkee that all the same proper guns." What he told me was that the war god is a fool, and he (the god) believed that what he saw was really guns—and consequently Peking was quite safe. I, for the first time, understood something of the frame of mind in which the Chinese regarded their idols. The gods were necessary institutions, but they could be easily cheated, and anything would do to gain their protection, so long as even a pretence of reverence was paid them. A similar frame of mind obtains towards another god—the sea god. All Chinese craft have an eye painted on either side of the prow of their boats, and many Chinese will not travel by a foreign steamer unless they see eyes painted on either side of the prow, or over the paddle-boxes. They have framed their belief after the manner of a syllogism in regard to the matter as follows:—

> " Suppose no got eye, how can see;
> No can see, how can savey;
> No can savey, how can walkee? "

The opening statement is not confutable:
" It is impossible to see without an eye "—
real, artificial, or painted, is not in the question. " If there is no eye, it is not possible
for the boat to know (savey) what direction
to take (walkee)." This legend is a com-
monly quoted bit of " pidgeon English," and
repeated to every visitor to China by old
Anglo-Chinese residents. Wishing to understand the import of this arrant nonsense, I
interrogated a Chinese in the matter and
said, " I cannot understand how a sensible,
practical people like the Chinese uphold such
beliefs as these. Why do they continue to
paint an eye on their ships? " He replied,
" That sea god he belong number one fooloo,
he thinkee that all proper eye." They humored the god, but they did not honor him.
Our forefathers propitiated witches in the
same way; many at times invoked their aid;
others, though disbelievers to an extent,
would say nothing against the witches in case
some calamity might befall them.

Christianity did not do away with these
beliefs in our country. The traditions of our
ancient heathen gods came down to us as our
witches, kelpies, bogie-men, &c., and to-day
we frighten our children with them. The
Chinese still set up their gods and propitiate
them, but all real belief in their powers has

gone, and sacrifice to the gods has become a mere mummery. We are not so far away from the Chinese way of thinking after all.

The transition from the old to the new China of to-day has been much in evidence during the past few years, and in nothing more markedly than in matters military. The bow and arrow, the official weapon of China, has been supplanted by firearms; but the transition died hard, and in several instances presented comical features. Even so late as 1894 the spectacle could be seen of sentries armed with bows and arrows mounting guard at the gates of the huge modern arsenal at Tientsin and at the Taku Forts at the mouth of the Peiho River. Within were Armstrong and Krupp cannon, modern quick-firing guns, repeating rifles, and all the munitions of modern war; without, a sentry carrying a bow and arrow.

But although " armed " with bows and arrows, even these were viewed with suspicion by their rulers. No one who has seen the Manchu soldiery practising with bow and arrow at the targets can ever forget the ludicrous spectacle. No archer hit the target, no archer dared to hit the target; it was as much as his life was worth. The Manchu authorities watched the proceedings carefully, never served out more than an arrow or two at a time, and care was taken that the point would penetrate nothing harder than a target of straw, rope, or canvas. They sagaciously reasoned thus: " If a man can hit the target, he can hit us." In other words, so little did the Manchus trust their own kinsmen that they were afraid of men who could shoot straight, and at all times took care that the weapon was incapable of causing a wound. A good shot might turn the weapon against his officer, and thereby wipe off old scores against the " oppressor." The men, therefore, dared not exhibit any skill, so the arrows went wide of the mark, or fell a long way short of the target.

With the modern foreign-drilled soldiers armed with rifles, blank ammunition was served out to them as a rule when they went to practise firing; this was partly no doubt for economy's sake, but partly to avoid the danger to the rulers of placing effective weapons in the hands of the soldiers. Even in the recent fighting around Hankow blank cartridges were supplied to the troops in many instances, and the cannon-shot used not infrequently consisted of wooden or clay balls shaped and painted to look like real cannon-shot. The practised economy in ammunition was not always on the part of the Government; the officers in charge of the am-

munition had to make their livelihood some-
how. As pay was small at best of times and
always uncertain in its bestowal, these officers
saw no way of earning a livelihood except by
deceit and fraud; hence the charges were
of sawdust or the bullets were abstracted and their place taken by stones, clay,
wood, &c.

This disregard of efficiency was due partly
to the desire for economy and to the fear of
arming the people, but largely to the traditional disregard and contempt in which the
Chinese for hundreds of years have held
prowess in the field of battle.

Although China has her mythology in common with the early history of all nations,
there is no doubt as to her antiquity as a
great and civilized power. Before the Chow
dynasty, which lasted for eight centuries and
terminated in 220 B.C., fable and fact are so
entwined that many are inclined to regard
the accounts of the *Three Emperors* as mythical. One of these " myths," however—
Fohy—some 2,600 years before Christ, intro-
duced organized government, the arts of
music and numbers, astronomical observations, and all that we understand by civilization in the home and in the national equipment. The *Five Sovereigns* succeeded the
Three Emperors, and after the sovereigns

came the period of the *Shang tyrants,* who
in turn were displaced by the *Chow dynasty,*
and with the Chow Emperors the definite history of China commences. The Chow rule
lasted for eight centuries, extending to the
year 220 B.C., and during that period Confucius lived and wrote. After his death in
477 B.C. civil war prevailed, and it was not
until A.D. 220, when the famous *Han rulers*
came into power, that the contending nations were again amalgamated as an empire.
The *dynasty of Tsin* commenced in 265 A.D.,
and it is presumed that the name China, or
Tsina, was given to the Chinese by the people
of India from these rulers. The Chinese
never had a name for their empire: they were
" THE people," the only people of the world,
and all other nations they regarded as mere
dependents, they themselves being the predominant inhabitants of the globe. In A.D.
416 the Tsin rule terminated, and the country
was divided into two, the southern portion
with its capital at Nanking, and the northern
capital in Honan.

In A.D. 585 the north and south were
blended for the first time with the capital
in Honan. The *Tang dynasty* in A.D. 618 succeeded to the throne, but lost it in A.D. 897.
Civil war ensued, and it was not until A.D.
960 that the *Soong* (Sung) *dynasty* was

raised to the throne. The Mongols, or Western Tartars, under Kublai Khan, invaded China and founded the *Yuen dynasty,* but their excesses and vices led to complete degeneracy, and the *Ming* (Chinese) *Emperors* succeeded to power in A.D. 1368, and ruled until the *Manchus, the Eastern Tartars,* usurped the throne in A.D. 1643, and only terminated their occupancy of it on February 15, 1912, owing to the efforts of Sun Yat Sen and his colleagues.

The Mongol or yellow race forms one of the three great types of the human family, and along with the Indo-European constitutes the population of Europe and Asia, with the exception of some of the negroid types in the Archipelago.

The Mongoloid type is stamped by several physical characteristics. The hair of the head is oval, not round; the skin is endowed with a less ample coating of hair than in the case of the Indo-European; the bridge of the nose is less pronounced, with the result that the skin of the upper eyelid forms a fold at its inner side, giving what is known as the Mongol type of face. It is usually said that the eye is oblique, but this is not the case. The fold of skin at the inner aspect of the upper lid gives rise to the apparent obliquity, and if the skin over the bridge of the nose is pinched up the fold, and so-called obliquity of the eye, disappears.

All European babies are born with a low or flat bridge to the nose and a fold at the inner side of the eyelid; the bridge of the nose gradually develops, until by the time puberty is reached the " bridge " has risen and the fold disappears. In the case of Mongols, however, the " bridge " does not, as a rule, develop; the eyelid fold remains, and the apparent obliquity of the eyes continues through life in consequence. Another facial difference between the Mongol and Indo-European is the presence and absence of " bumps " on the forehead. The European male at the age of adolescence develops " bumps " on the lower part of the forehead. These are not due to brain development, but to a separation of the layers of the bone of the forehead just above the eyes, leaving cavities occupied by air, which communicate with the nose. The elevations that result form the bumps so dearly beloved by the " head-reader," who endows them with varied forms of intellectual capacity. In the Chinese these air-cells are but slightly developed, and their features appear to occidental ideas as " baby-like." A " child-like and bland " aspect is natural to the features of the Mongols, not from the causes Bret Harte

would have us believe, but from normal eth-
nological developmental causes.

The marked development of the cavities in
several parts of the small European skull at
adolescence, when the voice " breaks," accounts for the more rugged outline of the
skull in Europeans as compared with Chinese;
and also for the depth of the male (bass)
voice in Europeans, compared with the most
tenor-like notes of the Chinese, especially
when singing, in which a high falsetto is the
rule. Of other physical Mongoloid characteristics one is a sturdy frame, and although
the bones are relatively small compared with
Indo-Europeans, yet is the muscular system
capable of great development. The gap also
between the canine (eye-tooth) and its neighbor in front is a characteristic Mongoloid
feature.

The question of the position of women in
China has been put to me by many women
who are interesting themselves in the political position of women in England. They
wanted to know Sun's attitude towards wom-
en's suffrage, and, although the subject is
rather a forbidding one to touch in England
at present, there can be no harm in describ-
ing the prospects of women in political matters in China. Sun's attitude is well described by Mr. Arthur Diosy in the London

SUN YAT SEN'S TWO DAUGHTERS
From a recent photograph

Globe in February, 1912. Mr. Diosy has
written several articles and letters and
spoken freely upon the part played by Dr.
Sun Yat Sen in the reform movement in
China. Mr. Diosy is deeply interested in
Chinese reform—a frame of mind inherited,
no doubt, for his father was Kossuth's secretary. No one is in a better position to declare his opinion than Mr. Diosy, for he has,
so far as Great Britain is concerned, alone
enjoyed with my wife and myself the privilege of an intimate acquaintance with the
great reformer, and of hearing Sun expound
his views on all matters appertaining to the
future of China politically, judicially and
socially.

Women in China have hitherto occupied
no place in the political horizon, apart, be
it said, from the dowager empresses in the
royal household—an example that cannot
be said to be propitious. Chinese women
were not supposed to learn to read and write.
A great difference indeed from the case of
the men, for every boy in China is taught
to read, write and count. In China for thousands of years this has been the case; yet in
Europe compulsory education is but a thing
of yesterday. In some nations of Europe
universal national education is still unknown,
and in some cases the proportion of persons

who can even now read is but about 30 percent. of the population. Although not, perhaps, given " school-board teaching " as we know it, yet is the Chinese woman educated in branches of household work which amount to little short of the marvellous in their excellence. In sewing work, in embroideries, in harmonizing of colors in dresses, table-covers, bed-quilts, petticoats, jackets, &c., the Chinese men and women are skilled beyond all other people, and their productions are frequently works of art which have long astonished the world by their perfection.

The position of the woman within the domain of the household is a superlative one; she rules absolutely, and, just as the dowager empresses have shown themselves capable of dictating terms to the Imperial household and edicts to the Empire, so does a woman hold sway within the jurisdiction of the family. The fact that men, who can afford it, have a plurality of wives must lead to friction, no doubt, at times; yet officially " No. 1 "—that is, the first wife—rules, and she has a voice in the selection of other wives if there are any. The mother-in-law, however, is the ultimate authority in the household. She must be obeyed always and at all times.

The hesitation of the Chinese women of the better classes as regards coming into the public gaze is an old-time custom observed to the letter. A male visitor seldom sees them, and in the street, when ladies go out, they are ensconced in a chair with the blinds drawn, so that they are completely hidden from view.

All Chinese ladies are supposed to have small feet; only women of the laboring classes allow their feet to develop naturally; but even in a relatively poor household it is an ambition to bring up one girl of the family at least as a " lady," and she accordingly has her feet bound. Mrs. Archibald Little has done a great work in trying to induce the mothers of Chinese girls to give up footbinding. The men declare they would like to see the custom done away with, but the women insist upon it, and it is owing to them that the children's feet are distorted. Sun intends, at the earliest possible moment, to legislate against the continuance of this cruel practice. This is no new departure, for ever since the tenth century A.D., when foot-binding is believed to have come into fashion, attempts have been made and edicts issued forbidding foot-binding, but with no very marked result. The Manchu women do not bind their feet; it is purely a Chinese custom. Children's feet are commenced to be " made small " at a very early age. The first bandage is applied so that the outer toes are bent under the sole, whereby in time the big toe is alone seen when looking down upon the upper surface of the foot. Later the second set of bandages are applied, and by these the foot is bent back so that the ball of the big toe well-nigh or actually does touch the heel. These bandages are applied throughout life, and the power of walking is reduced to a minimum. A maid or relative has to be at hand for all but the simplest and shortest movement, in order to keep the small-footed woman from falling. The Chinese argue that the custom of tight-lacing common amongst European women is much more detrimental to the physique than foot-binding in China. The evident answer to these comments is, that in China the children's feet are distorted by the mother before the children can say yea or nay, whereas in Europe the mother tries to prevent the daughter tight-lacing; the girl, in fact, before she tight-laces has attained to years of discretion, and need not do it unless she pleases. Women in all parts of the earth attach importance to the smallness of their feet, and the women of one nation deride those of another, as the French do the English, about the large-ness of their feet. To get the feet to appear small, therefore, boots and shoes are worn

by European women of a size and shape totally at variance with comfort, and the feet
become distorted and misshapen in consequence.

No Chinese woman with small feet ever al-
lows her feet to be seen by any one, not even
her husband, without the bandages, and similarly few European women are proud of
their bare feet, owing to the fact that they
have been distorted in consequence of wear-
ing boots or shoes several sizes, it may be,
too small. The origin of the idea that small
feet are a " thing of beauty " is lost in antiquity, but the result is seen to-day in the
small feet of Chinese ladies, and in the attempts to make the feet look small at all
hazards in Europe. Some say the distortion
of the foot is done in China to prevent the
women running away from their husbands
or straying far from their homes at any
time; others uphold them for æsthetic reasons, because the small-footed woman cannot
stand without swaying about, and she appears thereby more graceful—a " waving
golden lily." Why it is done in Europe is a
mere relic of barbarism, but it is a custom
which there would appear to be no sign of
disappearing from amongst us. The " small-
footed " woman in China, the " small-
booted " woman in Europe, will be with us

for many days, in spite of all efforts to uproot the evil.

Recently in China, chiefly through the influence and work of missionaries, Chinese girls are being taught to read and write. In several places they are being educated as doctors, and the fact that one can see many girls attending a medical course at Canton is a proof of the movement going on. A few Chinese women have found their way to the British Isles for the purpose of education. One of the most notable is Ronan-Woo (Mrs. Chang), who has just returned to China after attending the classes in the University of Aberdeen. Mrs. Chang is a niece of Yuan-Shih-Kai, and has done much to hasten reform in China. Yuan was the adopted son of her grandfather, and Yuan and her father were brought up as brothers together. Her grandfather was General Woo, who fought in the Taiping Rebellion on the side of the Manchus; her father was a magistrate, an advanced reformer, who persistently advocated change in education and politics for China. Yuan-Shih-Kai and his (foster) brother agreed that reform was necessary, but they differed in one point, as Yuan was always in favor of retaining the Manchus or the predominance of a sovereign, whilst Woo was in favor of a republic. So infatuated did Woo become with the story of the French Revolution that he named one daughter Joan of Arc and the other after Madame Roland. At fifteen years of age Mrs. Chang had read Carlyle, Stuart Mill, and Spencer. She went to Japan, where she met Sun Yat Sen and became his firm adherent. Mrs. Chang published a pamphlet styled the " Liberty Bell," which had a wide circulation in the Flowery Kingdom. Her uncle, Yuan, wanted Mrs. Chang to take up teaching at Tientsin in the province of Chili, of which he was at the time Viceroy, but she declined. At the London School of Tropical Medicine Miss Ida Khan, another Chinese lady, studied for a time and showed marked ability. No one who has met either Mrs. Chang or Miss Khan could but be impressed with the verve, the sound common sense, and the general air of capability which characterize both.

That the women of China are capable of playing an important part in their country's development is assured; that they will be asked to play a part is certain from Sun's statements on the subject. Many women have already helped the reformer's cause, several at the risk of their liberty and even of their lives, whilst some have even donned soldiers' uniform and fought in the ranks. Sun's intention is to give equal political rights to

men and women. It will not, however, be
universal suffrage, for strict educational tests
will be enforced in the case of both men and
women claiming the vote; and, as Mr. Diosy
says, it would not be surprising if there were
two Ministers of Education appointed, a man
and a woman, presiding over the departments
of male and female education respectively.

From earliest days in the history of China
education has been of paramount importance.
Attaining knowledge is the " be-all and the
end-all " of the *literati,* who constitute a very
large class of men in China. Theoretically,
and largely practically, advancement in Government employment is in direct proportion
to the amount of knowledge attained. Examination halls are, or rather were, a prominent
feature in the capital of every province. As
many as 10,000 students would assemble for
examination at a provincial capital. These
examination halls were permanent buildings.
A chamber or cell was assigned to each student; a high iron railing in front of the
chamber door prevented exit or entrance for
three days; the candidates took food in bas-
kets, and water was placed in buckets outside
the railings. Thither the best-trained pupils
in the province went for competitive examinations annually, and after a long and rigid
ordeal, carried out under supervision, a cer-

tain number of the best men were selected to proceed to the capital for competition for high posts in the Civil Service.

The subject-matter of the examination was the Chinese classics for the most part, and in addition, essays were required and poetry was not forgotten. The actual value of the knowledge requisite to pass these examinations seems to us perhaps worthless, but we must not forget that in our examinations for the highest posts in the Empire, namely, the Indian, Home, and Colonial Civil Services, the classics (Greek and Latin), essays, and a knowledge of English literature are of the first importance. One may ask how the knowledge of Chinese classics could make a man a good viceroy of a province; but similarly we may ask ourselves how an intimate knowledge of Latin and Greek can help our young men to deal out justice to a district in India or fit them for the multiplicity of administrative duties they are called upon to perform there. How well these young men manage Indian affairs is one of the marvels of government; and how well China was ruled through thousands of years by men similarly trained is a matter not to be lightly thought of in the present turmoil. One naturally asks how with an ignorant, corrupt, and effete government class in China the country was managed through all these centuries. The answer is that " the people ruled themselves."

The parental system so keenly upheld and rigidly taught by Confucius is the keynote of organization through the length and breadth of China. For thousands of years the Chinese, as distinct from others of the Mongol race, have been a peaceful people; well bred in the sense of being capable of restraint; loving learning for learning's sake, and withal possessing a well-ordered civilization. Etiquette, ceremonial and politeness have been looked upon as the essences of behavior. Respect for seniors, mindful of what is due to authority, and rendering due honor to parents has been instilled into the very fibre of their being ever since Confucius taught. A people thus trained and educated are easily governed; the government commences in the family and all else follows. Neither the change of dynasties nor the inroads of barbaric neighbors have altered the character of the Chinese by one jot or tittle, and it will be a bad day for China should these excellent traditions of their race be disturbed.

In the national life of China the schoolmaster plays a conspicuous and important part. Next to the parents the schoolmaster is held responsible for the children being well brought up. To such a degree is this the case, that should at any time after leaving school a young man misbehave himself the schoolmaster is held largely responsible for the misdemeanor. Although the boy may have left school several years, if he misbehaved upon the schoolmaster fell a meed of punishment, because he ought to have instilled better principles into the boy. Nor did the punishment cease here, for neighbors also suffered. A concrete example of the kind was told me by Dr. Sun Yat Sen himself. A son in an evil moment killed his father, when the punishment inflicted was as follows: Not only was the son beheaded, but also an uncle suffered the death penalty. The schoolmaster was exiled for 2,000 miles, and the neighbors, occupying the three houses on either side of the murdered man's dwelling, were condemned to leave their homes and not to take up residence within 1,000 miles of the village in which the murder occurred. A system of government of the kind may at times occasion an injustice to occur, but it has been effectual in keeping order in China.

The people govern themselves, and good behavior in the community is well-nigh ensured. That the teacher should be brought into the category of punishment appears, to our ideas, far-fetched, and were it acted upon

in Europe would bring home to our schoolmasters and our teachers of religion that the
nature of their teachings has a responsibility
which at present they are not supposed to
bear. In Britain religious and moral teaching is being denounced by the so-called " advanced " directors of public thought. According to many, there should be no moral
or religious teaching given to the children in
our schools; they should be allowed to choose
for themselves when they are old enough to
decide. Had the *régime* operative in China
been applied here, our schoolmasters and
clergy would be punished if any of their pa-
rishioners misbehaved themselves and came
within the criminal law of the country. A
wholesome doctrine which would serve us
well, for were every criminal traced to his native parish, and his clergyman held responsible for his departure from paths of rectitude,
it would stir our clergymen to become better
acquainted with the daily life of their parish-
ioners than they are at present. Apparently
the " advanced thinkers " of to-day would
do away with all form of prophylaxis against
the " disease of criminality "—for it is a disease—and the only thing we do is to treat the
disease after it has manifested itself. The
preventive measures—the business of the
clergy—have been largely removed, and it is

only when the signs and symptoms are pronounced that the " doctor "—in the shape of the policeman—is called in to treat the ailment.

The Chinese system is quite scientific, ours is pure empiricism, a mere tinkering with the disease we call crime. Prevention by moral training is at a discount, restraint is abrogated to the limbo of " old-fashionedness," and being sent to prison is often sufficient to stamp those who break our laws as heroes, or more often heroines, and the highway to win a martyr's crown. With this mode of regulating conduct in China, with every province an independent state, the idea of a republican or federal system of government is no uprooting of principles.

The monarchy has long been titular; its withdrawal is nothing more than the effacement of an idol or the heathen figure of a god. The Emperor has long been a mere " monarchical god," and just as the Chinese treat their war god, their sea god, and the numerous other gods which they set up to be dealt with as we treated witches and wise women—propitiating them when it suited us to do so, ridiculing them when we could afford to snap our fingers at them—the passing of the " son of Heaven," or monarchical god, when he misbehaves is no more to the Chi-

nese than the whipping of one of their household gods when he happens to disappoint
them, or even breaking the god in pieces and
scattering the fragments of the poor clay
image to the winds. Of all people the Chinese
are more ready to take up a federal system
of government than any other, for they have
practically been a republic, tolerating a monarchical deity in theory, but really proceeding
on federal lines for centuries. There is no
fear for the future, there are capable men
in China by the thousand; " potent, grave,
and reverend signiors," fit to rule a province
or direct an empire. Let those who cherished
the belief that a titular sovereign was necessary lay aside their fears, and with all confidence lend a hand to help this wonderful
people to a better state of government than
they have hitherto enjoyed.

In commerce the Chinese has been a potent factor ever since he became known to
the Western world. His commercial instinct
is acute, his honesty in commercial transactions has become proverbial. British bankers
in China tell us that in their banks the Chinese " shroffs " and " compradors " have
the handling of their dollars, and that in
many years of experience no dollar has ever
" stuck to the shroffs' or compradors' palm."
In the early days of commercial transactions

between Britain and China, when sailing-
ships took a year to come and go between
the countries, when there was no possibility
of written documents being drawn up and
duly signed, and the Chinese merchant's word
was all that the ship captain had to go and
come upon, there was no question of duplicity
amongst the Chinese, no going back upon
their word. When the ship captain returned
to England and told his employers that he
had made a contract with a Chinese to
ship another cargo of tea or silk a twelve-
month hence, they naturally asked to see the
agreement. Documents, however, there were
none, and the employers hesitated to believe
the captain as to the trustworthiness of a
contract of the kind. They did not know the
Chinese as the ship captain did, and he con-
tentedly undertook the long voyage to China,
knowing that the word of the Chinese
was as good as his bond, and that the bargain
he had made verbally was a secure one.
Should the market have gone against the
Chinese merchant, he would actually supply
the goods at a loss to himself, but the bargain
would be faithfully kept. Did the merchant
who undertook the contract die in the meantime, his relatives would be instructed to
carry out the transaction even if the family
lost thereby. Even with the " foreign devil "

the bargain was a consecration to be fulfilled
to the letter. Nor have the Chinese Government ever gone back upon their international
financial undertakings with Europeans. At
the very commencement of the recent outbreak of hostilities at Hankow and neighborhood, the leaders of the Reform Party posi-
tively stated that they would honor and respect all financial undertakings and international agreements contracted by China up to
the time of the commencement of hostilities.

Every one who knows China and the Chinese was conscious that this pronouncement
amounted to a bond; an undertaking which
would be conscientiously carried out. Yet did
the foreign financiers continue to '' flirt ''
with the Manchus, and persuaded the Press
that the Manchus, not the reformers, were the
winning side. The contemplated loan which
was being floated at the time of the outbreak
for the benefit of the Manchus was upon the
point of being '' put through,'' when wiser
counsels prevailed and advised postpone-
ment. Had the loan '' gone through,'' Europe would have been £10,000,000 poorer
to-day.

Had it been known that this rising was
no '' recurring row,'' but a universally preva-
lent national upheaval, no mere faction or
provincial rebellion, but instead a people de-

claring its mind, a movement that there was
as much chance of stemming as to thwart the
tide in its flow, there would have been no
attempts to smother its importance in order
to get the loan granted to the Manchu Government. Evidently none of the financiers
were sufficiently informed of the nature of
the recent rising, otherwise some of them
would have had the courage to grant a loan
to the reformers, and not to bolster up the
doomed Manchus.

Those who contemplated advancing the
loan in question sought information from
their Governments, and from every possible
source except the right one, namely, the people of China. These advisers pinned their
faith in the old *régime* continuing. They
clung to Yuan-Shih-Kai as drowning men to a
straw until the whole fabric crumbled beneath
them and a new China rose from the ruins.
Still was Yuan's the name, the only name
" officialdom " mentioned in this great upheaval; it persisted in believing Yuan would
be able to " save China " by preserving the
monarchy, and continued to lisp the name of
a man without power, except that thrust upon
him by the reformers, whom officialdom affected to despise.

Affairs have managed Yuan, and not Yuan
the affairs; as a diplomat he has long been

looked upon by the Chinese as a failure, but
regarded as a great soldier. They attribute,
rightly or wrongly, the loss of Korea to his
bungling. The death of the late Chinese Emperor, an ardent advocate for reform, would
not have taken place had Yuan not informed
the late Dowager Empress Yehonala of what
was contemplated. Had Yuan had foresight
or a spark of diplomatic genius, not to mention patriotism, in his composition, he would
never have allowed the late Emperor to have
been " removed "; he would have guided him
and advised him to keep quiet until nature in
due course had called the Dowager Empress
away, when he would have been left to rule
alone on modern lines, and thereby saved the
Manchus from expulsion and preserved a
monarchy for China. The Chinese say, " We
may grant respect to Yuan for his position,
but he is a product of Manchu rule and can
never be accepted whole-heartedly by the
Chinese. Sun Yat Sen is loved universally
and the people will follow his teaching and
principles devotedly."

Had Sun not been the great man he is,
moderate in council, sacrificing everything
for his country, with difficulty persuaded
from retiring to his native village and taking
up life as he began, there would have been
disturbances in the foreign relations of China.

Sun has, diplomatically, little to thank foreign nations for, except perhaps France. It was largely by French sympathy that China was allowed to work out her own salvation; and it is this Sun alone thinks of, not of the neglect, the slights, the churlish contempt for him and his doings displayed by " authorities." Whilst Sun has little to thank foreigners for, they, on the other hand, have much to thank him for. Their trouble in China arose from the exclusiveness, not of the Chinese people, but of the Manchu rulers. In the times of the Ming (Chinese) rulers the country was open to foreigners for travel, for commerce, for exploiting any new religion without let or hindrance. The masses of the Chinese, under the Manchus, have been taught to hate the foreigner; his presence has been upheld as a constant slight to the dignity of China; and even now were a powerful leader to direct a campaign of expulsion not all the might of Europe could repress it. Japan successfully defied the " might " of Russia, and altered the balance of power in the world. China has many resources and plans of campaign in addition to, and in place of, the power of arms.

Just now China would seem to be at the mercy of any nation or group of nations; it is well not to count too implicitly on this, but to be thankful that the spirit and principles which direct Sun Yat Sen are in the ascendant, for whilst he has power to guide and advise, there need be no anxiety. The people may prove too strong for Sun to control, when they find their great leader is regarded by foreigners as of no account in the national councils and that Yuan is alone deemed worthy of recognition; and the position of foreigners may become an awkward one. Letters from Europeans in high position in China which appeared in the Press in this country were ill-advised, and still further seek to belittle Sun Yat Sen at the expense of Yuan. The newspaper before me now, dated April 8, 1912, has an example of the style of article referred to. After devoting a column to Sun's intended doings in a sarcastic sense, the writer ends up by asking, " I wonder what stout old Yuan-Shih-Kai will have to say in the matter? " It is sincerely to be hoped that Yuan has the power and capacity his foreign admirers endow him with, and that he will carry out the work in the high position Sun has conferred upon him by resigning in his favor.

Even now foreign authorities smile at Sun and his doings; they almost invariably refer to his name apologetically, and any reference to his work or his statements ends up with

a slighting remark derogatory to him personally and laudatory to Yuan. It is a fetish,
a cult, that one who knows the world quite
understands. Sun cannot be bought or sold;
he cannot be driven from his purpose; he
despises publicity, and remains the same honest, simple, bewitching character, although he
has tasted of the highest position it is possible to think of.

Such a man is hopeless from a diplomatic
point of view; to financiers he is impossible;
he is the stumbling-block of company pro-
moters and an incessant vexation to the
would-be interviewer. Sun will never be popular with " authorities "; a man without an
axe to grind is impossible to deal with in a
committee, a council, a parliament, or a cabinet. His position resembles that of a doctor in public affairs; he has not only no axe
of his own to grind, but he brings forward
and supports schemes to improve the health
of the community and thereby injures his own
practice; he advocates hygienic schemes
which when developed may bring him to want.
Such a man, were he not a doctor, would
be called a fool; but the doctor is expected to
behave thus. So with Sun Yat Sen; he is a
patriot and nothing more, and not all the
wiles of financiers or the intrigues of diplomacy will ever cause him to deviate or make

him a party politician. It may be his training as a doctor that helped to bring him
under the ban, and caused the " authorities "
on China to pass him by as a negligible quantity or an insignificant cipher in China's
councils.

But if those in high places thus lightly regard a man of science, the people as a whole
hold him in high esteem, for in no way can
a nation be judged as to its position in the
scale of civilization better than by a study of
the position the art and science of medicine
holds within the realm.

As in other branches of activity, China relapsed from an early period of what may
justly be regarded as an advanced position
amongst nations in the art of medicine, to
a state of stagnation which has continued
until the present day.

We have it on fairly good evidence that
4,500 years ago the Chinese had an inkling at
least of the circulation of the blood; 3,000
years ago it is a fact that they performed
several operations skilfully and successfully;
as long as 2,400 years ago they had systema-
tized massage; and an accurate knowledge of
mercury as a drug existed a couple of centuries before the Christian era; and about the
fifth century A.D. serious operations, such as
removing tumors from the abdomen, trephin-

FIG. I

THE PANTAGRAMME, SHOWING THE
YANG AND THE YU, THE MALE
AND FEMALE ELEMENTS OF CREA-
TION, IN THE CENTRE

(See text)

ing the skull, &c., were frequently performed. At an early period specialism in medicine and surgery was in an advanced state. There were specialists for diseases of the eye, chest, abdomen, skin, women, children, bone-setters, dentists, pain-killers, bruise-curers, gland doctors, military surgeons, snake-bite curers, masseurs, corn-cutters, midwives, ship surgeons, faith healers, and miscellaneous doctors, in other words, general practitioners. So specialized, in fact, did the medical art become, that on external doctors or surgeons and internal doctors or physicians meeting in consultation over a case of an arrow-wound, the surgeon would nip off the arrow at the point where it protruded from the skin, but the part beneath the skin was left to the internal doctor to deal with.

Medical practice in course of time became mere adherence to ancient custom, and was completely subordinate to authority and tradition. Any one could set up as a doctor; a coolie, who through injury or laziness gave up manual work, would after a fortnight's study put up his " sign " and start practice. In the higher grades an apprenticeship was served before practice was commenced, and in the highest circle of all a knowledge of the points of the body at which needle puncture could be, and should be, made had to be displayed before the Royal Physicians in the capital. Hereditary instinct and inheritance was a passport to recommendation for a doctor, and as early as the Chow dynasty the public were warned against swallowing any medicine compounded by a doctor whose family had not been three generations in the medical profession. Chinese medical literature is voluminous, but with it all there is scarcely an item given that can be seized upon on which to found a theory or establish a fact.

The basis of things mortal finds expression in China in the figure known as the Pantagramme (Fig. 1). In the centre is the infinite void or universe, divided into two pear-shaped bodies by a double curved line, representing the male and female principle, the Yang and the Yu. Attendant upon these diagrammatic elements are eight symbols, of which four only have been interpreted. The uppermost, represented by three lines, is the male (Yang) symbol; the lowermost, by six short lines, signifies the female (Yu) principle; on the extreme right, consisting of a long central line and four attendant lines, is the symbol for Water; and on the extreme left, two lines with two intervening shorter lines indicates Fire. The four intervening sets of lines defied even Confucius to inter-

Female Reservoir   Male Reservoir

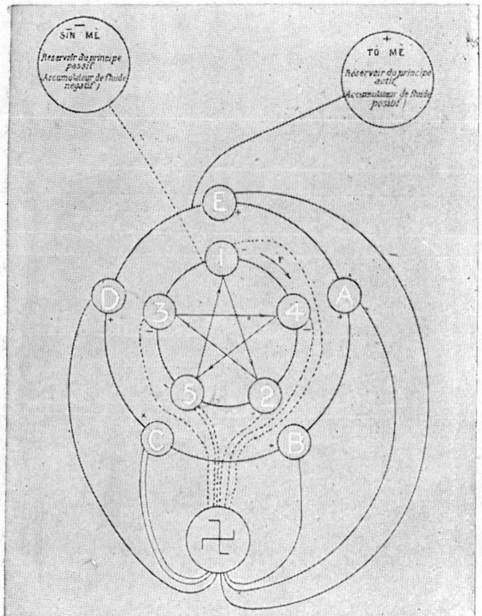

Fig. 2

SCHEME OF THE CONSTITUTION
OF MAN

(See text)

pret; and the fact that not only was the figure
in existence in his day, 447 B.C., but that the
actual meaning of it had been lost before his
time, shows the antiquity of this mythical
symbol. The diagram giving " the scheme
of the constitution of man " (Fig. 2) indicates a further advance in the knowledge of
the principles of physiology, although the
scheme is altogether incomprehensible to
modern observers. The idea seems to be that
there are two reservoirs. One, the inner, the
female or negative, is represented by the
inner circle, in which the " influence " passes
from No. 1, the Heart, to No. 2, the Lungs,
thence to No. 3, the Liver, and on to No. 4,
the Spleen, then to No. 5, the Kidney, and
finally, as the line indicates, it travels back
again to the heart.

The outer circle represents the male reservoir, in which A indicates the stomach; B, the
large intestine; C, the ureter or duct from
the kidney; D, the gall-bladder, and E the
small intestine. Below is the figure of the
Swastika, towards which the outlets of the
several organs concerned in the female reservoir empty, and beneath the Swastika the
ducts leading from the organs of the male
reservoir find exit.

The anatomical figure (Fig. 3) representing the position and relation of the different

organs of the body according to Chinese conception is scarcely in accordance with modern research. The heart will be readily recognized by its shape, and position; beneath
the heart is the diaphragm, the function of
which was not regarded as being that of
breathing as we have it, but served as a partition to keep down the fetid vapors which
emanate from the organs of digestion beneath
it. The body, in fact, is held to consist of
two regions: the part above the diaphragm—
the parlor or more genteel portion of the
economy; and the parts below—the kitchen
or culinary department of the body, and from
whence the fetid vapors arise. The more
prominent features of the anatomy, such as
the brain, the lungs, and windpipe, the gullet,
stomach, and intestines, &c., are to be recognized by a perusal of the picture, but the dis-
tribution of the large vessels connected with
the heart and several other items do not fit
in with modern anatomy.

All nations have had their periods of the
mythical in the healing art; and tradition has
affected humanity in medicine as in everything else; nor with all our " liberal " education have we got rid of mysticism and the
occult in medicine, and it is not likely we
ever shall. In the list of specialists in medicine in China in the remote past we find ex-

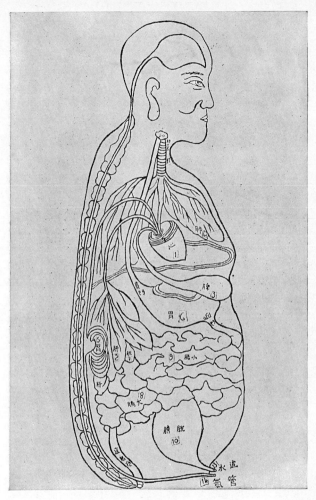

FIG. 3

AN ANATOMICAL FIGURE ACCORDING TO
CHINESE CONCEPTION

1. Heart; 2. Liver; 3. Gall Bladder; 4. Lungs; 5. Kidney;
6. Stomach; 7. Brain and Spinal Cord; 8 & 9. Intestines;
10. Bladder; 11. Windpipe; 12. Intestine; 13 & 14. Outlets.

amples in modern reversions to the original
type among ourselves. Bone-setters are with
us now, and are a class patronized especially
by the football fraternity, who go to their
bruise-curers as European women go to
Lourdes, or Chinese women to the Brass Mule
in Peking. Faith-healers of ancient China
are represented amongst us to-day by
Shakers, Christian Scientists, Theosophists,
or by one of the many beliefs and
practices which rise up with persistent
regularity under various names, only to
disappear before others still more soul-
absorbing in their appeal to the degenerates.
Let us see to the mote in our own eye before
posing and pitying the " poor deluded " Chinese for their ways and customs. As we
show signs of reversion in many quarters, the
Chinese on the other hand are going forward.
They are clamoring for education; the missionaries once held at arm's length are now
implored to teach philosophy, geography, history, science, or any department of modern
knowledge. A people to whom education is a
passion have become aware that the knowledge they have been allowed to acquire has
been limited to as much of the ritual of Confucius and other writers as their Manchu
rulers thought fit to let them have. The
repetition of these at schools led to nothing,

taught them nothing, and left them in ignorance. Suddenly a new era has dawned, the people are acquiring modern knowledge with avidity, and all prohibitions concerning the reading of books from which real knowledge can be acquired are removed.

Dr. Sun Yat Sen, whilst yet a boy, saw and understood the uselessness and senselessness of education in Chinese schools, and knew full well that an intimate acquaintance with the Chinese classics led to nothing. He longed for instruction in science, and it was this desire that brought him to the medical college in Hong Kong the moment it was opened; he was the first student and the first graduate. The sciences of botany, chemistry, zoology, &c., with which all medical teaching commences, opened new worlds to him, and every branch of study served to satisfy this son of intelligent China, a product of several generations of men whose brains had been famished by being deprived of the intellectual food which was their portion before the Manchus came and whilst yet the Mings held sway. Sun studied medicine as he has' studied everything else, ardently. The liberal education medicine gives has stood him in good stead; since his energies have been directed to other spheres of activity he has had to study international law, military tactics, naval construction, finance in all its departments, statecraft, and politics in all its bearings. He has visited many countries, and studied their institutions and modes of government. When residing with us in London, Sun wasted no moments in gaieties; he was for ever at work, reading books on all subjects which appertained to political, diplomatic, legal, military, and naval matters; mines and mining, agriculture, cattle-rearing, engineering, political economy, &c., occupied his attention and were studied closely and persistently. The range of his opportunities for acquiring knowledge has been such as few men have ever had, and the result is known to us. Sun Yat Sen is without doubt the man possessed of the widest and most liberal education in China to-day. Learning is the one quality that the Chinese respect above all others, and Sun's position to-day is due as much perhaps to his learning as to his unselfish patriotism and untiring efforts for his country's good.

IX

THE FIGHT WITH OPIUM

NO account of the Chinese Revolution can be accepted as complete that does not touch, however lightly, on the extraordinary efforts that China has put forth during the last few years to shake herself free from the insidious tyranny of the opium habit—a habit that in no small degree contributed to the inhuman inertia and deadly lethargy of spirit which to Westerners seemed to be permanently characteristic of the impassive Celestial. The story of China's deliverance from opium proves the contrary, and is one of the most inspiring that has ever been written of struggling humanity. It has moved even Cabinet Ministers to enthusiasm. Said Mr. Montagu, Under-Secretary of State for India: "Few reforms have been so marvellous in the history of the world as the determined, manful, courageous effort which the Chinese had made and were making to rid themselves of that terrible curse. They had made and were making progress which nobody, not even the Chinese themselves,

204

OPIUM SMOKERS

could have prophesied as being possible a few short years ago." This is warm praise, but no stronger than the facts justify, and those who still profess scepticism as to the permanence of the change that has come over China, and who confidently affirm that the revolution and the Republic are alike of mushroom growth, to pass away as swiftly as they came, cannot do better than study this chapter of the history of the " unchanging East "; for most clearly does it demonstrate that, once the Celestial has really resolved on his objective, once his mind is made up about it in earnest, then he brings to bear on its attainment an unsleeping energy that nothing can resist, and that, as some one put it, " leaves the world lost in astonishment."

This has proved to be the case with opium. Five years ago Great Britain negotiated what has been called the " ten years' agreement " with China. Put shortly, its terms were these: We, on behalf of India, undertook to reduce the amount of opium sold in Calcutta on Government account for export to China by 10 per cent. every year until the traffic had finally ceased. There was, of course, an equivalent, indeed a much greater, undertaking on the part of China. She covenanted to diminish her own production

coterminously with our supplies. Think
what this meant! Opium-smoking had become the national vice of China, as certainly
as alcoholism is ours. The habit had per-
meated every class of society. The idea that
only the low-grade Chinese indulges in the
opium pipe is, of course, fictitious. The business man, the Court official, the nobles—all
were addicted to a habit so deep-rooted as
to make its eradication seem almost impossible, a habit as common as is tea-drinking
here. The Chinese Government said, in effect, that it must cease within ten years.
Small wonder that the edict was food for
smiles everywhere—except in China. The
most determined enemies of the opium traffic
thought that the Government were courting
disaster by attempting to achieve in a decade
what it might take two or three generations
to accomplish. Scarcely any one dared to
hope for success, and it seemed that China
had entered on an impossible task. Quite
apart from the fearful hold which the opium
habit had gained over hundreds and thousands of Chinese, there was another factor
which made its eradication most difficult—
the loss of revenue to the small farmer, to
whom the cultivation of the poppy was a valuable " side line." Opium, it must be remembered, is extremely portable. The

farmer found it easy to carry to market. He could put the whole product of several fields on his back and sell it readily and profitably. The Government proposed to deprive him of this most welcome addition to his income. More, all officials who took opium were to be turned out of Government employ. Opium dens were to be closed and opium-smokers held up to public ridicule. Nearly every one prophesied failure. The very missionaries who had carried on a crusade against opium for years sadly shook their heads. Failure seemed inevitable.

And then what happened? Travellers reported that, whereas opium-smoking was once so common a vice that you could see men puffing a pipe at their own doors, two years after the edict those who smoked, smoked secretly. Lord William Gascoyne-Cecil, in his fascinating book, " Changing China," tells of the extraordinary difference those two years made in the aspect of the land. On his first visit the country, as seen from the railway between Hankow and Harbin, was exquisite with the white and pink crops of poppy, " resembling the transformation scene at a variety theatre." But on his next journey every poppy had disappeared. The edict was being enforced! Men were going to the missionaries asking for some cure or relief from the terrible suffering that the cessation of the opium habit brought. Others died from the strain. Morphia syringes began to make their appearance, for many sought relief in hypodermic injections. But the elimination of the poppy went on. In Yunnan, the province which formerly had the largest proportion of poppy growth, opium gave way to silk and cotton cultivation. In other districts the production of cereals enormously increased. In Chekiang, the Statistical Secretary stated: '' It is satisfactory to be informed that the decrease in the importation of rice at Ningpo, which amounted to the value of 3,300,000 Hk. taels ($2,500,000), and which by so much reduced the total of native imports, was made good by the produce of lands lately rescued from the poppy in the prefecture of Taichow.''

In many provinces total prohibition was resorted to, and the punishment that followed its infraction was death. The success of these repressive measures and the immensity of the undertaking of the Chinese Government may be realized by a glance at the extremely interesting map here produced by kind permission of the Society for the Suppression of the Opium Trade. [1]

[1] The three sets of figures are (1) the estimates of opium cultivation in each province contained in the Report on Opium

All this was done only at the cost of immense pecuniary sacrifice. India has, so far, actually gained by the diminution in the growth. For, so far as she is concerned, the only reasonable computation proceeds on the average receipts before the recent agreement was made. On that basis the net annual revenue from opium sent to China amounted to £2,489,000, and the first year's loss to the Indian revenue should have amounted to £248,900, and in three years to thrice that sum, viz., £746,700. Indeed, it was understood that the Indian Government, looking forward to the gradual reduction during ten years, calculated on eleven or twelve millions sterling as likely to be China's contribution to India's opium revenue before the trade was abolished. Whilst, according to the most reasonable computation, India's revenue from opium sent to China should, during those first three years of the agreement, have been £1,991,200, £1,742,300, and £1,493,400 respectively, the result has been far otherwise. Instead of steadily diminish-

in China, prepared at the British Legation in Peking in 1907, and published in the official White Paper, China, No. 1 (1908); (2) and (3), the estimates of opium cultivation in 1906 and 1908, presented to the Shanghai Opium Commission by the Chinese delegation. Since then, further great reductions have been made.

ing, her revenue from opium sent to China
has been largely increased as follows:—

	Total Opium Receipts	From China
1908-09	£4,648,700	£3,867,700
1909-10	4,418,200	3,637,200
1910-11	6,460,000	5,697,000

That is to say, that the Indian Treasury, instead of receiving as the result of the first
three years of the agreement the sum of
£5,226,900, has actually received the sum of
£13,183,900, or something like two millions
sterling beyond her reasonable hope for the
whole ten years. Indeed, India's revenue
from opium sent to China this last year is
far greater than in any year for a long time
past. The sales have diminished by 15,300
chests, and yet the revenue has enormously
increased. Whence has the increase come?
The explanation is only too easy. The diminution of China's output by seven and a half
tenths has raised the price of Indian opium
along the coast of China to an enormous degree. In a multitude of places there is now
not a grain of Chinese opium to be had, and
the wealthier confirmed smokers are ready
to pay 300 to 500 per cent. for the Indian
drug to relieve their horrible craving.
China's eagerness to be rid of the national

curse is being paid for at a ransom price.
And lest any should say that these high
prices for Indian opium are just the fluctua-
tions of the market, we have only to note the

MAP TO SHOW WHAT CHINA HAS DONE

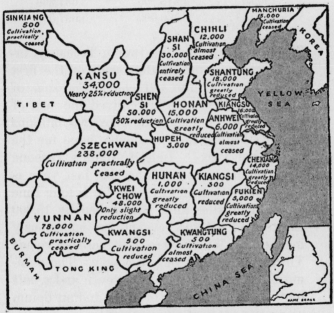

MAP OF OPIUM PRODUCTION IN CHINA.

extraordinary efforts made by the holders of
opium for other countries to bring that opium
to China, efforts that are entirely opposed
to the spirit of the agreement.

Let us look now more nearly at China's

pecuniary sacrifice over against India's gain.
India computed her own normal loss at
£248,900 a year, or in the three years £746,-
700. And the two elements involved in China's
loss are (1) all the surplus that India has
gained in these three years, amounting in all
to £7,957,000, and (2) whatever may be esti-
mated as the value of the opium relinquished
for the sake of the national welfare. She
has given up, not 15,300 chests, like India,
but 438,800 chests, and computing this
for a moment at what was the Indian
opium price at the beginning of the
agreement, we find that it amounts to
£746,000 (India's loss on 15,300 chests)
$\times 28 \dfrac{(438,000)}{(15,300)}$, or £20,888,000; and
adding the two items together we have
the enormous sacrifice of £28,845,000. It
may be said that this is putting the value of
Chinese opium at too high a rate, but if we
take five millions sterling from it we still
have the enormous sum of over £23,845,000.[1]

No one can doubt that China will recover
these lost millions. But who will deny that
their sacrifice, at a moment in her history

[1] For this analysis of the financial aspects of the question,
and for the figures given in support thereof, the authors are
indebted to Dr. Maxwell, the Chairman of the Board of the
British Anti-Opium Societies.

when she needed money more than ever before, when in fact her exchequer was drained,
does not prove her grim earnestness?
Surely the time has passed for despising a
people with such vast reserves of energy,
such unconquerable resolution.   Enfeebled
and corrupt China may have been.   Not so
now.   She has crushed the poppy beneath her
feet and at last she is aroused.

X

THE FUTURE OF CHINA

WHAT is to be the future of China?
On what lines will the great Republic of the East develop? Will
she retain any, and which, of the characteristics that marked the Celestial Empire—that
Empire which for centuries seemed imper-
vious to change? Now that at last change
has come, what will be the consequences?—
first, upon the situation in the Far East;
then upon the world at large—the world that,
accustomed to discount China as a supine
giant whom nothing could rouse, now has to
realize that her awakening liberates a force,
strange and incalculable, that must be reckoned with.

These questions are of profound, of far-
reaching importance. No one who has tried
to realize the stupendous industrial and commercial possibilities that hinge upon the
opening of China; no one who has even
faintly comprehended all that a Yellow Peril
might mean to Europe, can fail to grasp
their significance, for upon them, or rather

upon the answers of history during the next half-century, it may well be that the whole fabric of our civilization depends. To try and anticipate history would be foolish indeed. Prophecy, we know, is ever the most gratuitous form of error. But from the many perplexities of the situation at least one or two cardinal facts stand clearly out—facts that properly considered may serve in some measure as pointers for the future. They indicate unmistakably in what respects the new China will, and must, differ from the Empire that has gone by for ever.

First, then, between the old China and the new there is one great gulf fixed. The Chinese of yore, he whose neck was bowed beneath the yoke of the Mongol or the Manchu (foreigners both), was taught to despise the soldier, and despise him he did. Learning, scholarship, these he revered, even when they were wholly divorced from the realities of life and given over to the memorizing of dead classics. But the soldier, the man who went down fighting against odds for his country, was akin to the barbarian, at best a necessary evil. A Chinese writer explains this inferiority thus: " First," he says, " comes the scholar: because his mind is superior to wealth, and it is the intellect that distinguishes man above the lower order of beings and enables him to find food and raiment and shelter for himself and for other creatures. Second, the farmer: because the mind cannot act without the body, and the body cannot exist without food, so that farming is essential to the existence of man, especially in civilized society. Third, the mechanic: because, next to food, shelter is a necessity, and the man who builds a house comes next in honor to the man who provides food. Fourth, the tradesman: because, as society increases and its wants are multiplied, men to carry on exchange and barter become a necessity, and so the merchant comes into existence. His occupation— ' shaving ' both sides, the producer and the consumer—tempts him to act dishonestly, hence his low grade. Fifth, the soldier stands last and lowest in the list, because his business is to destroy and not to build up society. He consumes what others produce, but produces nothing himself that can benefit mankind. He is, perhaps, a necessary evil.''

All this the Revolution has changed. Never again will the Chinese despise the profession of arms or seek to degrade valor. It was from no mere accident, but by a deliberate act of great significance, that Sun Yat Sen inspected the Chinese Fleet the day following his selection as President of the Provisional Republic. Again, almost the first proclamation that Republic issued was to call for a conscript army. The fact is that China has had hammered into her the old lesson that a country can know nothing of real dignity, let alone security or peace, unless she is prepared to fight for them with her own right arm, and that scholar, farmer, tradesman, and merchant alike, all are dependent on the soldier for freedom to follow their avocations. During the past few years, the proud Celestial has had heaped upon his head humiliation after humiliation from hands he despised. Consider for a moment how the events of the past decade and a half must have appeared to him.

First came the challenge to his suzerainty over Korea. Then followed the war with the Japanese—China's pupils till recently—whose claims were regarded with amused contempt, and by whom the Chinese were so soundly thrashed that they had to appeal to the European Powers to protect their territory. Their pride was soon to sustain a deeper wound. Two German missionaries were murdered by a mob of fanatics. Nothing would placate the inexorable German but a part of the Celestial Empire itself, and Kiao-chou was ceded. Then came the Boxer

Rising and the terrible vengeance exacted by
the Powers for the outrages committed—the
sack of the capital, the loot of cities, the dishonor of women as the allied troops passed
through the country burning, devastating,
pillaging.

Yet their cup of humiliation was not full,
for the Russo-Japanese War broke out—to
be fought not in Korea, not in Russian, not
in Japanese territory, but in Manchuria,
which belonged to China, with whom neither
combatant was at war—an unmistakable in-
dication to the world at large that the Celestial Empire had ceased to count!

Small wonder that these things should
have burnt themselves into the soul of the
Chinese, and that even before the Revolution
he should have set about the task of reorgan-
izing his army in earnest. "Is there no
higher power than that?" asks the highly
cultured young lady in "Major Barbara,"
pointing to a shell. "Yes," is the answer;
"but that power—the shell—can destroy the
higher powers as a tiger can kill a man.
Therefore it is necessary that man must master that power first." And in some such
spirit the Chinese realizes that the culture
of his beloved *literati* and the revered tombs
of his ancestors will not be proof of themselves against the invading foreigner. We

may take it, then, that the first essential difference between the China of to-day and the defunct Empire is that the Republic will strive to become a great military power.

Already English and American officers are on their way to train the revolutionaries, already the latest type of quick-firing guns have been despatched to the Republican Government. Consider for a moment what a prospect this opens up! China has a population four hundred million strong. Once her people become proficient in the use of arms, she can face fearful losses in battle with comparative equanimity—losses that would stagger any combination of European Powers. It may be said, it is still widely believed, that the Chinese cannot be got to fight, that he is at heart a coward, and that he will never stand punishment like European troops. Facts do not support this theory. Those who have seen the Chinese in action under competent leaders speak of him as a magnificent soldier. Lord Elgin praised most highly the Tartar cavalry. Gordon often could not find words to express his admiration of his own Chinese troops, and his diary teems with tributes both to their bravery and to that of the rebels he was fighting. Of one battle, he said that never in his experience of the Crimea had he witnessed anything like the hand-to-hand fighting for fierceness and determination; and when we recall some of the battles of the Crimea this praise ought to be conclusive as to the mettle and endurance of the Chinese soldier. The English officers who commanded the Wei-Hai-Wei regiments and those who led the Chinese volunteers at the siege of Peking spoke as warmly as Gordon, and it is reported (so says Lord Gascoyne-Cecil in his " Changing China ") that the Chinese soldiers at the siege of Tientsin would carry the wounded out of the range of fire when no European was forthcoming for the task.

The fact is that the almost open contempt of the Chinese for soldiering has misled European observers into thinking him a skulker and a runaway. But the battlefield proves the contrary. The contempt was only part and parcel of a general mental attitude —an attitude that has passed completely away. Says Mr. Putnam Weale in his book " The Struggle Round the Far East ": " The general military organization in China is now undoubtedly far better than it has ever been before. At such places as Kiu Kiang, Soochow, and Foochow, the writer has recently seen battalion after battalion (each the nucleus of a future divisional organization) turn out, relatively speaking, well clothed, well armed, and exceedingly well drilled.'' The same authority quotes a secret memorandum setting forth the details of the Chinese Army, according to which, '' just before the great autumn manœuvres of 1906, provision had been made for the creation of 18 major units or divisions, divided up on the Japanese-German brigade and regimental system, and therefore comprising 36 infantry brigades, or 72 regiments (making a total of 216 infantry battalions, 72 squadrons of cavalry, and 152 batteries of artillery). Of these corps ten divisions were almost complete before the end of 1906, while eight divisions consisted merely of skeleton corps.

'' Shortly after the memorandum was drawn up, the organization of an additional division was begun in North China by Yuan-Shih-Kai, making the seventh division in North China; while the Canton division, several battalions of which have already been recruited, was also comprised in the general scheme, being designated No. 20, and was ordered to bring the skeleton regiments up to full strength as quickly as possible. Further, the transfer of troops to Manchuria began on a big scale in April, 1907, and will now be followed by the creation of new corps.

Probably four divisions will at first be detailed for duty in Manchuria; and it may therefore be assumed that the immediate work of Lu Chun Pu, Minister of War, will be the completion of an army of twenty-four divisions, which will number some 300,000 men of all arms on a peace footing, and which will possess, when the artillery parks have been fully organized, no less than 1,216 field and mountain guns.''

This may be taken as indicating the maximum of China's immediate military resources. But it is of value for the moment only. Nothing is more certain than that the Republicans intend to organize the military resources of China on a vast scale and under the most efficient guidance they can secure.

What will be the effect of this new force upon the balance of power in the Far East? How far will it menace the hold on China that the Powers have secured? Will it, for instance, ultimately mean notice to quit to Europe?

Ultimately, it may. At present there is no possibility of such an event. But in other directions the army that China can now muster will almost certainly lead to far-reaching consequences. For instance, as Mr. Putnam Weale truly points out, if China can create a force strong enough to convince the occu-

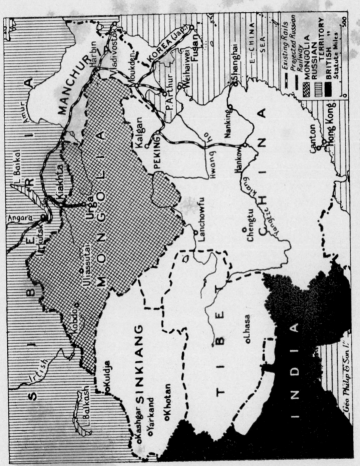

OUTLINE SECTION MAP OF CHINA
AND THE TERRITORY SURROUNDING IT

pants of Manchuria that she is in a position to resume the complete mastery of her outlying territories, " a new series of evacuation treaties may have to be prepared." It is scarcely credible that a demand for these treaties would lead to any difficulties that statesmanship cannot surmount. The day has passed when the Powers found Chinese diplomacy impossible. Indeed, if there be one result of the Revolution more certain than another, it is that the relations between China and Europe have entered definitely upon a new chapter, free from the irritating absurdities, the suspicions and hostilities of the past and to be characterized by candor and cordiality. The Reform Party in China look to Europe for help and encouragement in their task of reconstructing a mighty nation, and once their aims are appreciated they will not look in vain. One cloud there is on the horizon, however, no bigger than a man's hand. In one of his most recent speeches in Canton, Sun Yat Sen referred very briefly to an old controversy—that touching the question of extra-territoriality —and as it is practically certain that more, much more, will be heard of the matter, it may be as well to state shortly in what the difference consists.

The facts are these. When, in 1842, the

Chinese had been hopelessly defeated by
Britain, they signed the famous treaty of
Nanking. This provided for the compulsory
cession of the Island of Hong-Kong, the
opening of not only Canton but Amoy, Foochow, Shanghai, and Ningpo as treaty ports,
the location of a British Consul in each port,
and, most necessary but most humiliating of
all to China, the recognition of the extra-
territorial rights of all foreigners, so that
no matter what their crime, they could not
be tried by Chinese courts, but only by their
own Consuls. This treaty contributed so
much to the opening of China that Dr. S.
Wells Williams characterized it as " one of
the turning-points in the history of mankind,
involving the welfare of all nations in its
wide-reaching consequences." That may
have been the case.

None the less the Chinese have always
bitterly resented its terms. In fact, these
extra-territorial rights are one of the chief
sources of irritation against foreigners, for
they not only imply contempt for China,
but make foreigners a privileged class. Said
Minister Wen Hsiang in 1868: " Take away
your extra-territorial clause, and merchant
and missionary may settle anywhere and
everywhere. But retain it, and we must do
our best to confine you and our trouble to

the treaty ports." Unfortunately this is a cause of resentment that Western nations cannot immediately remove. While we can understand the resentment of the Chinese magistrates as they see their methods discredited by the foreigner, it would not do to subject Europeans and Americans to Chinese legal procedure. The answer of Mr. Wade, the British Minister, still applies:—

" Experience has shown that in many cases the latter (*i.e.*, the law of China) will condemn a prisoner to death, where the law of England would be satisfied with a penalty far less severe, if, indeed, it were possible to punish the man at all. It is to be deplored that misunderstandings should arise from a difference in our codes, but I see no remedy for this until China shall see fit to revise the process of investigation now common in her courts. So long as evidence is wrung from witnesses by torture, it is scarcely possible for the authorities of a foreign Power to associate themselves with those of China in the trial of a criminal case; and unless the authorities of both nationalities are present, there will always be a suspicion of unfairness on one side or the other. This difficulty surmounted, there would be none in the way of providing a code of laws to affect mixed cases; none, certainly, on the part of England; none, in my belief, either, on the part of any other Power.''

Meantime, as the Hon. Frederick Low, United States Minister at Peking, wrote to the State Department at Washington, March 20, 1871: '' The dictates of humanity will not permit the renunciation of the right for all foreigners that they shall be governed and punished by their own laws.''

There can be no doubt whatever that so long as the corrupt and degrading system of justice that characterized the Manchu *régime* persisted, it was not possible for civilized countries to adopt any other attitude than that of rigid insistence on their extra-territorial rights. The old Chinese criminal code differs so widely from our own, it is, according to Western notions, so capricious and inexplicable, that obviously Europeans would not live under its harsh and antiquated provisions. But now the question arises, or it will soon arise, as to whether this attitude does not properly belong to ancient history, for in the recasting of Chinese institutions none, it is certain, will be reformed more drastically than the judiciary. The day of the corrupt and impossible mandarins is over.

Who will take their place? Students and lawyers, trained, not only in Chinese uni-

versities, but at Western seats of learning—
men who have taken their degrees at Oxford
and Cambridge, at Harvard and Berlin, and
who will administer laws based not upon
obscure customs, and drafted centuries ago,
but passed in a Parliament representative
of modern China and with the experience of
the world to guide its deliberations. We
must not forget that perhaps the greatest
triumph achieved by Sun Yat Sen and his
colleagues has been that while they have
carried on, under the extraordinary circumstances we have described, an incessant warfare with the Manchu despotism, they have
never lost sight of the fact that a day would
come when it would be absolutely necessary
for them to set about the work of reconstruc-
tion, and accordingly, as the impending collapse of the old *régime* became more and
more apparent, Sun Yat Sen succeeded in
persuading the rich and influential among his
supporters to send the brightest spirits of
the younger generation to be educated outside China. There is something decidedly
impressive in the quiet confidence and
strength of a leader who, as he directs the
pulling down of a doomed edifice, takes steps
to raise another in its place, and the pre-
science of the man who has for twenty years
directed operations against the Manchu des-

potism will be in nothing more apparent than this: that now the crash has come he has his men ready for all the positions of trust and danger on whose fitness the State must depend. This is true of the Army, of the Navy, of the Magistracy, and it is certain that, with a reconstituted bench, whose *personnel* is unexceptional, administering a modern and scientific system of law, the Republic will press on the Powers the demand for the abrogation of these extra-territorial treaties. China, when weak and decadent, accepted them only under pressure. China conscious of her own immense reserves of strength is not in the least likely to suffer them a day longer than she can help.

How will China enforce this demand? She can bring to bear on Europe a most powerful, albeit indirect influence—the influence of trade. The great objection to the Manchu dynasty outside China was that it hampered commerce at almost every turn. It needed not one, but many wars to get European business men ordinary commercial facilities, and, as we have seen, the industrial resources of the country have not yet begun to be developed. It will be the policy of the Republican Government, not to continually restrict and harass trade, but, subject to certain conditions, to facilitate by all means in their power the opening up to the industrial nations of the earth of the greatest market for their goods that the world can afford.

It is certain, even from the speech of Sun Yat Sen to which we have referred, that the price she will demand for this is the cancellation, probably under a time limit, of the extra-territorial clauses, giving in return treaties and concessions of infinitely more importance and value.

For there can be no " possible probable shadow of doubt " that the revolution in China is to be the precursor of one of the greatest industrial " booms " that the world has ever seen. Consider first the neglected mineral resources of the Flowery Land. The world has only faintly realized the value of these deposits. Huge reserves of anthracite coal and vast quantities of iron are two of China's most important assets. Both have been proved: neither has been worked. True, for centuries the Chinese have been busily engaged in working the coal outcrops in Hunan, and in other parts of the Empire. But how? By means of shallow pits and the most rudimentary appliances for dealing with water, which finally overwhelmed them. True, also, that recently numerous attempts have been made upon the part of various financial groups to develop the vast deposits of coal on modern lines.

There was, for instance, the famous Peking Syndicate, formed to exploit the metalliferous areas of the two rich provinces of Honan and Shansi, provinces which, according to the scientist traveller, Baron Von Richthofen, contain enough coal and iron to keep the world busy for two thousand years. The prospects of the syndicate were, therefore, excellent. But what took place? The shares, it is true, went to a premium on the Stock Exchange, but the actual coal and iron raised were a negligible quantity. Disturbed conditions prevented any operations until 1902. Then there were difficulties with the Chinese Government, who procrastinated as only Celestials can.

Finally, so it is alleged, it was discovered that the original contract of the Peking Syndicate was defective, inasmuch as the English and Chinese texts differed in some essential particulars, and it was, unfortunately, never agreed which text was to be the authoritative one. There have been other syndicates formed with prospects just as alluring, with histories just as barren of results to every one except the lawyers. It was essential, in fact, to the development of China that a new spirit should animate her

Government, that a new faith should quicken
the pulse of her people, and the inevitable
has happened. Both the Peking Syndicate
and the basket method of mining belong to
an era that has definitely closed, and the first
care of the Republican Government, once it
has provided for national defence, will be to
organize upon modern lines the development
of the national wealth whose neglect was
alone sufficient to condemn the Empire. Let
us see for a moment what this means to
China. "While in Teng-Chow-Fu," says
Mr. Brown, "we witnessed a pathetic ceremony. There had been no rain for several
weeks. The kaoliang was withering and the
farmers could not plant their beans on the
ground from which the winter wheat had
been cut. The people had become alarmed
as the drought continued, and they were
parading the streets bearing banners, wear-
ing chaplets of withered leaves on their heads
to remind the gods that the vegetation was
dying, beating drums to attract the attention of the gods, and ever and anon falling
on their knees and praying, ' O Great Dragon,
send us rain! ' It was pitiful. This country
is fertile, but the population is so enormous
that, in the absence of any manufacturing or
mining, the people even in the most favored
seasons live from hand to mouth, and a

drought means the starvation of multitudes.''
Obviously a people living almost exclusively
on agriculture and disdaining mining ¡and
manufacture must become inured to a standard of living that appears incredibly low to
the Westerner, with few comforts and with
their very food liable to constant menace.
Inevitably the industrial awakening must
check this impoverishment of the people.

Let it be remembered that a direct result
of this impoverishment is infanticide, the
greatest blot on the Chinese escutcheon, for
it should be noted that this horror is preva-
lent only where grinding poverty obliterates
natural affection. Only in the famine districts may we read the words '' Girl babies
must not be drowned here.''

The effect of the industrial awakening will
be felt far outside China. It will provide the
European and American exporter with such
a market as trader never dreamed of. With
the Republic China has entered definitely
upon a course of commercial development,
and we have only to reflect for an instant
upon the vastness of her population to realize that this way lies an economic revolution
such as the world has never seen. No effort
will be required on the part of the Chinese
to enter industrial life, for which alike their
instinctive capacity for craftsmanship and

their sense of discipline eminently fit them.

Once the Chinese finds his standard of life is rising, once his wants increase and multiply so that his consumption becomes considerable, obviously his country will offer unequalled opportunities for the expansion of trade. Already there are indications that point in this direction. Modern inventions, more varied foods, articles of comfort formerly unsuspected of the Celestial, these have already made themselves known in China. The peasant is no longer content with the wretched tallow candles and " oil lamps " with their wicks floating in cups; he wants kerosene instead of bean oil, and he is learning to buy American lamps, and thus Chinese households are being rescued from the misery of semi-darkness. In Canton the narrow streets are brilliant with houses lit with German chandeliers and lamps—cheap perhaps, but infinitely superior to those they have replaced. Not only are new lamps for old demanded, but there is everywhere in China evidence of the liveliest dissatisfaction with the wretched housing conditions, and for the mud roof of a generation ago bright red tiles are being substituted. The impact of Western ideas has created a host of new demands of which Europe is already feeling the benefit.

The old days when China bought next to nothing from the West are over. At a banquet given by the foreign Ministers to the Emperor and Empress Dowager in the famous Summer Palace outside Peking a few years ago, the guests cut York ham with knives from Sheffield, and drank French wines out of German glasses. And not merely the aristocrats and the wealthy, but the people themselves are touched by the new spirit. The children that went naked are being clothed, and already thousands upon thousands of sewing-machines are buzzing in countless Chinese homes. Fathers and mothers are learning to vary the eternal monotony of " rice diet." They are learning the superiority of wooden floors to ground encrusted with filth, of good roads to tortuous paths through heaps of putrid garbage.

In a word, China is becoming civilized, and as a purchaser of Western goods she will easily outdistance all competitors. The change set in prior to the revolution, which will enormously quicken the pace.

Cotton and flour mills have been springing up in various parts of the country. Silk filatures fitted with modern plant are everywhere on the increase. Small native-owned iron foundries and machine shops with European machinery are being established along the coast, river, and rail, and during the decade 1896-1906—a period that included two wars, several famines, and many sporadic outbreaks—the net value of the foreign trade of the country increased 80 per cent.— from 366,329,983 taels in 1897 to 646,726,821 taels in 1906.

" If these things are done in the green twig, what shall be done in the dry? " Remember, the above increase was effected in the teeth of the opposition of a Government bent upon hampering trade in every possible respect. The contrary will be the policy of the Republic, whose leaders realize to the full that they are responsible to countless millions whose only escape from abject poverty lies in the expansion of trade. And they will seek to extend that trade, first and foremost, by the provision of such a system of railways as will liberate the immense mineral resources of China and make their development a commercial possibility.

The provision of railways is to China an absolute necessity of her complete industrial awakening. Without them her minerals cannot profitably be worked. There are, it should be borne in mind, no roads to speak of in the interior of China. Ruts have been made by the passing of generations of feet and wheels—ruts that are either thick with dust or fathomless with mud. Add to this one other consideration—the bewildering vastness of the territory—and we realize at once the paramount importance of improved transit. What has been done thus far in the direction of providing China with railways? The first railway ever built in China, that laid down in 1875, was, as we have seen, destroyed by the Government. It was six years before it was followed by another attempt, a line from the Kaiping coal-mines to Taku, at the mouth of the Fei-ho River and the ocean gateway to the capital. Later this line was extended, and now forms part of the Imperial Railway, belonging to the Chinese Government, though with bonds issued on it to the French and American capitalists who financed its working. It was not till 1895 that any concessions to build railways, much worth counting, were granted by the Chinese Government. Then they were issued rapidly, and, according to the *Archiv für Eisenbahnreisen* of Germany, the total length of the railways in use in China was about 742 miles, an aggregate so trifling as to be ridiculous, while lines of the very greatest importance, whose very construction will require years of constant work, are " projected " and remain so.

"HEADS AND TAILS"
A Street scene in Shanghai.   A festal occasion

What has caused the delay? In part it is due to the inherent defects of the old order, the almost endless procrastinations, the interminable delays, the stubborn hostility to foreign syndicates—for all of which and for a hundred other offences the Manchus are to blame.

On the other hand, we must recognize that no little blame attaches to the "frenzied finance" which has used railways in China merely as a bait for unwary speculators, without making any serious effort to place them on a sound footing. Worse even than the merely obstructive policy of the Chinese Government has been this: that, as Mr. Putnam Weale explains, "no effective control has been exercised by the Government over the European syndicates, with the result that the whole system of railway building has been bad from first to last." Constructional expenses have too often been made simply enormous so as to allow commissions of inordinate size to line the pockets of those who have been successful enough to receive building concessions. In no other part of the world would syndicates have been permitted to float loans without first submitting to the Government of the country definite surveys and building tenders, which would afford a check on capital expenditure and make the concessionaires, and not the Government, liable for any expenditure not expressly specified in the final contracts. In the case of the Shanghai-Nanking Railway, the original estimates have been exceeded by nearly three-quarters of a million sterling.

In this particular case there is a keen dispute as to where the blame should be laid, but speaking generally, there can be no possible doubt that the railway development of China has been grievously retarded, as much by unscrupulous concessionaires as by the supineness of the Chinese Government. It needs no great penetration to discern what the policy of the Republican Government will be, for, while on the one hand they will do everything in their power to encourage capital with which to inaugurate a really adequate system of railways, yet they will end once for all the system, whereby groups of men and interests, not primarily associated with railway building, come into the market to exploit the Chinese by raising to an absurd figure the capital cost of the railways built.

Railways, in fact, will, after national defence, be the first care of the Chinese Executive, which will leave no stone unturned, first, to secure the capital for their construction; secondly, to see to it that not a penny is wasted. A stupendous task indeed, but well worth the effort.

As Mr. Brown says: " It would be impossible to describe adequately the far-reaching effect upon China and the Chinese of this extension of modern railways. We have an illustration of its meaning in America, where the transcontinental railroads resulted in the amazing development of our western plains and of the Pacific coast. The effect of such a development in China can hardly be overestimated, for China has more than ten times the population of the trans-Mississippi region, while its territory is vaster and equally rich in mineral resources. As I travelled through the land, it seemed to me that almost the whole northern part of the Empire was composed of illimitable fields of wheat and millet, and that in the south the millions of paddy plots formed a rice-field of continental proportions. Hidden away in China's mountains and underlying her boundless plateaus are immense deposits of coal and iron; while above any other country on the globe, China has the labor for the development of agriculture and manufacture. Think of the influence, not only upon the Chinese but the whole world, when railways not only carry the corn of Hunan to the famine sufferers in Shantung, but when they bring coal, iron, and other products of Chinese soil and industry within reach of steamship lines running to Europe and America. To make all these resources available to the rest of the world, and in turn to introduce among the 426,000,000 of the Chinese the products and inventions of Europe and America, is to bring about an economic transformation of stupendous proportions.''

SUN YAT SEN
With Autograph

A STATEMENT AND AN APPEAL BY SUN YAT SEN *

"TO *the Friends of China in the United States of America:*—

" While officially I am not compelled to speak of Chinese affairs and can in no direct sense be a mouthpiece for the Government of the Republic, I feel that it is my bounden duty to speak quite fully regarding matters in which I am deeply concerned to the end that certain misunderstandings prejudicial to the interests of my country may be cleared.

" Perhaps I would not feel this justification were it not for the fact that with my own eyes I have read in American and British journals many misstatements of fact, particularly regarding my own relations with the head and heads of the Chinese Government and of certain factions of my countrymen. All manner of rumors and reports have been

* Reproduced by permission from New York *Sun*, Sept. 24, 1912.

sent by telegraph and mail from the different ports of China and Japan to the European and American publics, and I would not be surprised if the intelligent opinion of the Western peoples was to the effect that we here in China are rapidly preparing to undo the good that has been done.

" I can readily understand that certain acts of those in authority might be understood to mean that revolution or rebellion was pending in parts of the Republic. I am not called upon just now to say whether I fully approve of some of the recent acts of President Yuan Shih-k'ai. Perhaps I approve, perhaps I do not; that is a matter wholly personal, and has no bearing—or, at least, should have none— upon political matters and conditions generally.

" The relations between President Yuan and myself are personally very cordial. It is true that we do not agree upon all matters of public policy, but our differences are those which the world expects to find among its public men. It would be remarkable, to say the least, if a set of public men could be found in any country who were of one mind in all matters of public concern.

" I believe I can safely say that upon one matter of first importance all the leaders in China are of one mind: The best good of the country. As to how this may be attained is quite another matter, but we are all striving and working for the one meritorious and noble end.

" No one thinks of a civil war in the United States simply because Mr. Taft, Mr. Wilson and Mr. Roosevelt do not agree upon matters of public policy. Each of these gentlemen is certainly a true American and a patriot of a very high order. Yet there are—if my knowledge of American affairs is worthy— many great and vital issues upon which they disagree totally.

" May it not be so in China?

" I have but within a few hours returned from a visit to the capital; the city which, if foreign journals are to be credited, I hardly dared visit because of the personal danger I would run! It is too bad; it is wicked indeed that such ideas should be published broadcast. Great injury is thus done our country and the cause for which we have so long striven. Both are given a setback in the eyes of the world.

" During my visit to President Yuan in June I told him very frankly my ideas upon many important matters that were then to the fore. We discussed at length the six Power loan, as it had been called, and the terms upon which it should be made and accepted. We also went into the matter of the relief of distress, the organization of political parties, the teaching of civil science to the people, the disposal of Government mines and lands, the project of opening vast tracts of agricultural lands for settlement and other matters of import.

" At that time President Yuan gave out a very complete statement of his views on many of these questions, and while his expressed opinions were his own they embodied very largely my own views on the various topics. Almost to the last word of that statement my own views were in accord with those of the President.

" If the foreign correspondents at Hongkong, Shanghai, Pekin and other places would but make an effort to ascertain the truth on questions involving the welfare of the nation or the policy of the Government, or would diligently search out those officials who are in a position to give them facts, there would be less conflict of opinion in foreign countries regarding Chinese matters.

" It is for this reason that I am willing, even anxious, to make this statement. I desire that my country and countrymen, and the relations of President Yuan and myself, be placed properly before the intelligent peoples of Europe and America. In this age public opinion is ofttimes more potent for the advancement of good or the accomplishment of evil than fleets of warships and divisions of armies.

"I wish to go on record once and for all as saying that in spite of the efforts, past or future, of the enemies of the Chinese Republic there will be no civil war in our country. China has been credited with having been a 'sleeping nation' for centuries, and in a certain sense—in many senses, in fact—the phrase has been correctly applied. But our enemies must not count too confidently upon China being asleep to-day. Her leaders are awake to the needs of her people, to the call of the twentieth century, to the hopes and ambitions of the present.

"We understand too well that there are certain men of power—not to include for the present certain nations—who would view with a greater or lesser satisfaction an internal rupture in the new republic. They would welcome as a move toward the accomplishment of their own ends and designs a civil war between the provinces of the north and the south; just as, fifty years ago, there was applause in secret (in certain quarters) over the terrible civil strife in the United States.

"Americans of to-day who were alive in those dark days of the great republic will remember the feelings in the hearts of the people—the bitter and painful thoughts that arose from the knowledge that foreigners were hoping and praying for the destruction of the American Union.

" Had the war been successful from the South's standpoint, and had two separate republics been established, is it not likely that perhaps half a dozen or more weak nations would have eventually been established? I believe that such would have been the result; and I further believe that with the one great nation divided politically and commercially outsiders would have stepped in sooner or later and made of America their own. I do not believe that I am stating this too forcibly. If so I have not read history nor studied men and nations intelligently.

" And I feel that we have just such enemies abroad as the American republic had; and that at certain capitals the most welcome announcement that could be made would be that of a rebellion in China against the constituted authorities.

" This is a hard statement to make; but I believe in speaking the truth so that all the world may know and recognize it.

" However, foreign ill wishers may as well understand first as last—perhaps better now —that the men who are at the forefront of

Chinese affairs are a unit for the Republic as established and cannot be brought, individually or in factions, to oppose the onward march of the Chinese nation. Neither flattery, fear, intrigue nor gold has power to make the leaders of the new China, nor any one of them, turn back the hopes, wishes and aspirations of our people.

" As I have said in the beginning of this statement, I am not called upon to speak officially for the Government of China. President Yuan Shih-k'ai is the head of the nation, the strong, worthy leader of his people, and I am not authorized to speak for him, for his Cabinet or for the National Assembly; but I believe I am voicing the sentiment of a united and unanimous people when I warn trouble makers, at home or abroad, that the Chinese nation has joined the great family of republics to remain a member thereof at whatever cost or sacrifice.

" Let not one word which I have uttered be construed as being even remotely a hint that the China of the new order is opposed to foreigners or to legitimate outside interest in the country's welfare. The very opposite is the case; for we welcome the missionaries, the men of trade and the capitalists and scientists of the other nations.

" In proof of this it may be cited that Pres-

ident Yuan Shih-k'ai has already selected
three eminent foreigners to aid him in his
work: One a jurist, the second a journalist,
the other a college professor. Another eminent man, an American diplomat and one of
China's foremost friends, is desired for a high
post at the capital, and a formal request has
already been made both to the United States
Government and to the gentleman concerned.

" Why are these men desired? Simply because they are men of wisdom, who have
shown in the past that unselfishly they have
the interests of China at heart. They are
men of the calibre of the late Sir Robert
Hart, for a quarter of a century at the head
of the finances of China. Sir Robert, an
Irish-Britisher, became the most trusted as
he was the most efficient and influential of
' Chinese.'

" No man because of his nativity or creed
will be barred from service under the Republic. Now, above all times, my country needs
the assistance of the world's best brains.
But enemies to the State will not be tolerated;
and upon this point the Chinese people, high
and low, are a unit.

" Perhaps it is almost superfluous for me
to say that the most pressing need of China
to-day is her establishment upon a sound financial basis. The country is in need of a

large sum in order that the wheels of government machinery may revolve without friction. Alarmists have said because the proposed loan has not been quickly negotiated that the Republic was in dire danger of collapse. There is not a shadow of reason for this assertion, for while it is true that the problem of the establishment of the new order of things would be very much less complex if our Treasury were amply supplied, it is also true that with the means at its disposal the Government has accomplished great things; and it is but a question of time—six or eight years perhaps—that, even without a great national loan, the affairs of the country will be upon a satisfactory financial basis.

"It must be remembered that while China has millions of very poor people (and hundreds of thousands who are constantly but a few days removed from possible starvation) there are also millions of people capable of paying taxes in amounts greater or less, and that when the new system of taxation is put into operation in all parts of the country the various governments, city, provincial and national, will be well supported.

"Now that the country is again at peace, excepting in certain remote and unimportant districts, I look for a big increase in commerce, domestic and foreign, with consequent well being in agriculture, manufacturing and the various other industries. With the people everywhere working, with peace at north, south, east and west, the country is bound to be prosperous and the Government stable and substantial.

" It should be remembered also that China, in spite of her reputation for poverty and famine, is really a very rich country in natural resources. Tradition, belief and superstition through the centuries have conserved the minerals of the country, the great quarries of granite, marble and onyx and the vast forests of valuable woods in the south and southwest. Experts have made reports and have told me personally that the coal lands still untouched are of a value quite unfigurable, while the iron, copper and zinc hills are pronounced by French experts to be the most promising ever operated anywhere.

" When it is understood that all these properties, as well as over a hundred millions of acres of fertile agricultural lands, are the unquestioned property of the Government, it can readily be seen that, except for immediate and transient needs, the country is far from being in a state of insolvency.

" The President, his Cabinet and the National Assembly—backed as they are by the intelligent sentiment of united China—are determined that these properties shall not pass from the hands and control of their rightful owners, the people of China. Concessions and leases will be granted, have in some instances already been made and granted, but the title shall not pass from the Treasury.

" Therefore China, although thousands of years older than any of the other living nations to-day, is younger than the youngest of them so far as the richness of her mountains and the fertility of her virgin lands are concerned.

" I wish to speak briefly now about one other matter, my attention being drawn to it by the publication of a sensational cable in England to the effect that myself and my followers were insisting—under a veiled threat of civil war—that the capital be removed from Pekin to the ancient seat of government, Nankin.

" Frankly and avowedly I am in favor of a more central location for the capital, believing that Pekin is too remote from the large centres of population. It is as if the seat of government of the United States were located at Augusta, Maine. Washington is far from occupying a central location, but it at least has the advantage of being about midway of the Atlantic coast line of the United States. A relative position for China's capital would be about Shanghai or Nankin, and it is because of this that I have advocated the change —not because, as has been foolishly asserted, that I feared in its present site it would be more likely to capture by the Japanese!

"Japan is our nearest great neighbor and we expect to live on the most friendly terms with her. Old animosities have been forgotten. It will be to Japan's benefit if China grows in progress and prosperity; and I cannot be made believe that Japan has any other feeling toward us than one wishing us a long and rich future.

"My recent visit to Pekin was not made for the purpose of stirring up trouble or discord. It was, on the other hand, to assure President Yuan that many sayings attributed to me were not only untrue but without the slightest foundation in fact. I have not only confidence in his loyalty and ability and believe him worthy of the firmest support, but I repledge myself to devote my best and every effort to aid him in the great and noble work he has undertaken.

"It is my earnest wish that this statement be given the widest publicity possible."

SUN YAT SEN.

Nankin, China, August 27, 1912.